T0328657

Cambridge Elements ≡

Elements in Experimental Political Science
edited by
James N. Druckman
Northwestern University

DEFECTION DENIED

A Study of Civilian Support for Insurgency in Irregular War

David S. Siroky
University of Essex

Valery Dzutsati
University of Kansas

Lenka Bustikova
University of Oxford

CAMBRIDGE
UNIVERSITY PRESS

CAMBRIDGE
UNIVERSITY PRESS

University Printing House, Cambridge CB2 8BS, United Kingdom

One Liberty Plaza, 20th Floor, New York, NY 10006, USA

477 Williamstown Road, Port Melbourne, VIC 3207, Australia

314–321, 3rd Floor, Plot 3, Splendor Forum, Jasola District Centre,
New Delhi – 110025, India

103 Penang Road, #05–06/07, Visioncrest Commercial, Singapore 238467

Cambridge University Press is part of the University of Cambridge.

It furthers the University's mission by disseminating knowledge in the pursuit of
education, learning, and research at the highest international levels of excellence.

www.cambridge.org
Information on this title: www.cambridge.org/9781009016452
DOI: 10.1017/9781009025539

© David S. Siroky, Valery Dzutsati, and Lenka Bustikova 2022

First published 2022

A catalogue record for this publication is available from the British Library.

ISBN 978-1-009-01645-2 Paperback
ISSN 2633-3368 (online)
ISSN 2633-335X (print)

Defection Denied

A Study of Civilian Support for Insurgency in Irregular War

Elements in Experimental Political Science

DOI: 10.1017/9781009025539
First published online: March 2022

David S. Siroky
University of Essex and Arizona State University

Valery Dzutsati
University of Kansas

Lenka Bustikova
University of Oxford and Arizona State University

Author for correspondence: David S. Siroky, david.siroky@gmail.com

Abstract: How can researchers obtain reliable responses on sensitive issues in dangerous settings? This Element elucidates ways to use unobtrusive experimental methods to elicit more truthful answers to risky, taboo, and threatening questions in dangerous social environments. The methods discussed in this Element help social scientists to encourage respondents to express their true preferences and to reduce non-response bias, while protecting them, local survey organizations, and researchers. The Element is grounded in an original study of civilian support for the jihadi insurgency in the Russian North Caucasus in Dagestan that assesses theories about wartime attitudes toward militant groups. We argue that sticky identities, security threats, and economic dependence curb the ability of civilians to switch loyalties.

Keywords: experiments, civil war, civilians, insurgency, Russia, Caucasus

ISBNs: 9781009016452 (PB), 9781009025539 (OC)
ISSNs: 2633-3368 (online), 2633-335X (print)

Contents

1 Introduction

Dagestan: the most dangerous place in Europe.[1]

In situations of captivity, the perpetrator becomes the most powerful person in the life of the victim, and the psychology of the victim is shaped by the actions and beliefs of the perpetrator.[2]

How can we safely acquire reliable responses for research on delicate issues in dangerous settings? This Element demonstrates how social scientists can reduce incentives among respondents to conceal their true preferences by applying unobtrusive experimental methods designed to elicit truthful answers for threatening, risky, and taboo research topics.[3] In this Element, we explore civilian support for Islamic rebels in Dagestan, an issue about which an open discussion could potentially get respondents and interviewers killed, imprisoned, or kidnapped. Studying dangerous and difficult topics in unstable societies requires significant sensitivity, but it is feasible, as we suggest, using unobtrusive experimental methods. We illustrate how it can be done by integrating an original study of civilian support for the insurgency in the Russian North Caucasus (in Dagestan) with a broader discussion and comparison of various experimental methods for exploring sensitive subjects.

What determines civilian support for rebels? Our framework characterizes civilians as "hostages" to their respective rulers, with no exit options, hence the title *Defection Denied*.[4] Sticky ethnic and religious identities, economic dependence, and security concerns curb the ability of civilians to switch loyalties. Since civilian attitudes largely follow from these social structures, direct victimization increases support for the perpetrators of violence.

This leads us to expect intimidation tactics, such as direct victimization, to be associated with *increased* support for perpetrators, such as jihadis, who abuse civilians. Civilians have limited exit options: their loyalties and identities are very sticky. Furthermore, their security, well-being, and access to resources depend on local networks. Therefore, once they find themselves in one of the warring camps, they cannot easily "defect" (i.e., change their assigned label and

---

[1] L. Ash, "Dagestan: The Most Dangerous Place in Europe." *BBC News*. November 24, 2011. www .bbc.com/news/magazine-15824831.

[2] J. L. Herman, *Trauma and Recovery: The Aftermath of Violence – From Domestic Abuse to Political Terror*. New York: Basic Books, 2015, p. 75.

[3] Removing incentives to conceal the truth, which this Element addresses, is a somewhat distinct problem from creating incentives to *reveal* the truth, which often requires imposing some penalties on respondents. The indirect questioning techniques discussed in this Element create incentives to reveal but do not remove incentives to conceal. Another problem is nonparticipation, which is distinct from the issue of non-response, and can lead to a different kind of selection bias.

[4] "No Exit" draws on the title of Jean-Paul Sartre's 1944 play, *Huis Clos* (No Exit).

switch sides). Civilians are locked into silos under the loose control of either the insurgency or the pro-Russian counterinsurgency forces. As a result of these constraints, civilian victimization does not engender resistance, but instead solidifies loyalty, dependence, and obedience. In doing so, we explain why direct civilian victimization may serve as an effective tool of social control in irregular wars.

The insurgency in Dagestan had two goals: independence from Russia (a nationalist goal), and implementation of Sharia law (a religious goal).[5] Both aims rendered them enemies of the Russian state and also put them at odds with secular elements of Dagestani society. Still, like most insurgencies, they had a civilian support base. We naturally wondered which Dagestani civilians supported or opposed the rebels and why. However, as will become clear over the course of this Element, using regular surveys with direct questions on support for the insurgency would have put respondents and enumerators at significant risk. It would also most likely have produced an unacceptable level of non-response and sensitivity bias.

Indirect questioning techniques have a long tradition in social sciences, mostly psychology and sociology, and in survey methodology research (Bernard, Johnsen, Killworth, Robinson 1989, 1991; Chaudhuri and Christofides 2007, 2013; Greenberg et al. 1969; Miller 1984; Raghavarao and Federer 1979; Swensson 1974; Warner 1965). In this Element, we will discuss a variety of alternative approaches and also mention some of the many applications of these techniques across the social sciences. Our focus will be on showing why we decided to use, and in the end how we used in the context of a very unfriendly research environment, one of the most serviceable of these techniques: the endorsement experiment.

In pursuit of better understanding civilian support for the insurgency in Dagestan, we considered various unobtrusive experimental survey techniques. In Section 4, we assess their strengths and weaknesses. Using direct questioning as the baseline, we compare four techniques specifically designed to reduce sensitivity bias. The techniques discussed include: (1) the unmatched count technique (list experiments), (2) the randomized response technique, (3) sealed envelope methods, and (4) endorsement experiments. We ultimately elected to design a series of endorsement experiments. Instead of asking respondents whether they support a sensitive actor, the survey instrument therefore asks whether respondents support a policy that is – through randomization – sometimes "endorsed" by a sensitive actor and at other times just endorsed by a

---

[5] On the persistence of sticky identities in warn-torn environments, see Chaisty and Whitefield 2017.

neutral control of "some people." To put it differently, instead of probing the support for an "actor" (rebels, for example), the surveyor asks whether the respondent endorses something the "actor" stands for, thereby indirectly measuring the respondent's support. We will present and explore the endorsement experiment approach – and several other techniques – in greater depth throughout the rest of the Element.

An endorsement experiment is a fancy name for something that is intuitive to understand and grounded in decades of research in social psychology (Petty, Cacioppo and Schumann 1983; Chaiken 1980; Cialdini 1984; Petty, Wood, and Kallgren 1988). Endorsement experiments detach the respondents from the sensitive actor (e.g., rebel group) issue or item by asking them about their support for policies rather than about their support for the sensitive actors themselves. In the experimental version of the survey instrument, respondents are told that the sensitive actor "endorses" the policy, whereas in the control version, there is no mention of the sensitive actor at all – just the policy.

One of the key reasons the "endorsement" technique works is that it lessens incentives for respondents to conceal their true preferences. Therefore, it reduces sensitivity bias and non-response – the two key problems when probing delicate issues and tricky social actors. In the treatment version, the respondents' support for policy hides support for the actor, and for this, respondents are spared the potentially adverse consequences of expressing support directly. Randomization of respondents to control and treatment groups and differences in the levels of endorsements revealed by the experimental technique enable us to extract latent levels of support for the sensitive actor without actually asking directly about it. By exploiting this "evaluation bias in human judgment" (Rosenfeld, Imai, and Shapiro 2016, p. 3), the endorsement experiment aims at revealing the true attitudes of respondents in regard to a host of sensitive actors and taboo topics. Evaluation bias means that people generally value the same thing more if it is linked to a positive person or thing.

One of the first political science applications to use endorsements focused on race relations in the USA (Sniderman and Piazza 1993). More recent articles that used endorsement experiments examined support for the Taliban and the International Security Assistance Force (ISAF) counterinsurgency forces in Afghanistan (Lyall et al. 2013), and support for using violence, conditional on climate change effects in Kenya (Linke et al. 2018). We focus on civilian support for the insurgency in Dagestan to illustrate how endorsement experiments can be used to advance research and knowledge of highly relevant but difficult-to-probe social phenomena, while simultaneously providing protection to the human subjects involved in the studies, both respondents and enumerators.

To understand why direct survey questions were not feasible in the first place, let us briefly describe the context of our study. In 2015, when we implemented the survey in Dagestan, threats to civilians came from three sides: the highly potent and abusive pro-Russian government forces, and two competing insurgency movements with related but divergent radical ideologies: one a homegrown Islamic separatist organization, the Caucasus Emirate (a.k.a. Imarat Kavkaz – IK); the second, a branch of the Middle Eastern extremist organization Islamic State (IS) (a.k.a. Islamic State in Iraq and Syria – ISIS or Islamic State of Iraq and the Levant – ISIL).[6] The government's aggressive counterinsurgency campaign in this peripheral region meant that eliciting truthful answers to questions on support for the insurgency would represent a serious challenge, regardless of the methodological approach adopted. In 2006, the Russian government officially introduced Article 205.2 into the country's Criminal Code, which outlaws any material or *verbal* support for rebels, and therefore puts in danger respondents who express any support for the insurgency.

The law explicitly forbidding any verbal support for the insurgency and making it a punishable crime rendered any direct questioning impracticable – and, indeed, irresponsible. For comparison, in very dangerous circumstances in Afghanistan at the time of the counterterrorism campaign, voicing support for the Taliban was not a crime and, in some quarters, may have been even safer than expressing affinity with the government and ISAF. While Afghanistan is a failed state, Russia is an authoritarian state, where laws exist and are enforced, but are habitually bent to suit the needs of the government. This implies substantial uncertainty about the consequences for any individual who speaks their mind openly on many topics.

At the time of our research study, rebels both from IK and IS were struggling for influence, and civilians were being targeted on a regular basis. This

---

[6] Although IK did not cease to exist, IS integrated some former IK fighters, and one new *jamaat* decided to join IS instead of IK. The "competition" between the groups also occurred in Syria and online. As our survey took off, IS established a branch in Dagestan. See "IS Claims Deadly Shooting in Russia's Caucasus: SITE." *Middle East Eye*, December 31, 2015. www .middleeasteye.net/fr/news/claims-deadly-shooting-russias-caucasus-site-1293027991. On this period, see Mairbek Vatchagaev, "What Caused the Demise of the Caucasus Emirate?," *The Jamestown Foundation, Eurasia Daily Monitor*, June 18, 2015. https://jamestown.org/program/ what-caused-the-demise-of-the-caucasus-emirate-2/. See also Mairbek Vatchagaev, "The Islamic State Is Set to Replace the Caucasus Emirate in the North Caucasus.," *The Jamestown Foundation, Eurasia Daily Monitor*, January 8, 2015. https://jamestown.org/program/the- islamic-state-is-set-to-replace-the-caucasus-emirate-in-the-north-caucasus-2/. Yet even years later it continues in a diminished form. See Valery Dzutsati, "Despite Demise of Insurgency, Authorities Still Wary of Its Remnants." *The Jamestown Foundation, Eurasia Daily Monitor*, May 20, 2020. https://jamestown.org/program/despite-demise-of-insurgency-in-north-caucasus- russian-authorities-still-wary-of-its-remnants/.

unfavorable context arguably made it all the more critical to utilize some form of indirect questioning; thus, after examining the various options that we discuss further in Section 4, we determined that endorsement experiments were best suited to this topic and setting. While this Element focuses on war zones and other violent contexts, we mention a variety of other applications in the social sciences and hope that our discussion will inspire some readers to use these methods in their own research and in other contexts.

No indirect questioning technique can eliminate all risk to respondents and enumerators or completely assuage their fears. However, scholars can take a number of steps at the design stage of their research to increase the validity of their inquiry and to protect human subjects. One of the least explicitly discussed steps is the importance of integrating qualitative domain knowledge and area expertise with survey techniques, which ensures that we understand how locals are likely to perceive the questions, particularly in terms of the risks that providing truthful answers may entail for them and their families. Qualitative research is important when we craft the questionnaire, but is also virtually indispensable when it comes to interpreting the results.

When designing our study, we integrated our own qualitative knowledge and expertise, but also consulted with a local survey organization in the North Caucasus to design the questionnaire in a manner that would minimize risks to both respondents and enumerators, and would ensure that we were using the correct terms for the concepts that we sought to capture in our study. We teamed up with a well-known scholar and member of the Russian Academy of Sciences, Dr. Khasan Dzutsev, who until recently ran an established survey organization in the region with a reputation for academic and ethical integrity that has been doing survey work in the North Caucasus for three decades. Although our partners went to great lengths in order to protect the identities of respondents in order to minimize risks, no research of this kind can eliminate all risks.

Cronin-Furman and Lake (2018) discuss the ethical implications of such research and have provided extensive guidelines on how to conduct ethical research in fragile states and dangerous settings while mitigating risks.[7] Weak states present particular challenges for Western researchers who possess advantages that can facilitate research (primarily economic resources), but also potentially create exploitative and dangerous situations.[8] Power imbalances and perverse motives create hazardous incentives for all participants and unethical environments for researchers, especially when it comes to accessing victims, ex-combatants, and vulnerable populations (Cronin-Furman and Lake

---

[7] For other work in this area, see Campbell (2017); Kapiszewski et al. (2015); Sriram et al. (2009).

[8] Access to humanitarian networks to evacuate Western researchers rapidly if a security situation deteriorates is an option that is not available to local researchers.

2018, p. 608). In repressive states, complying with government regulations can present tradeoffs between the need to avoid surveillance and harassment and the expectations of research transparency.

It is equally important that dangerous situations and populations should not be "exoticized." Although far from a panacea, collaborating with respected local research partners is an important strategy for reducing risk and conducting ethical research in conflict-ridden areas and dangerous settings. Frequently, such organizations and partners play a critical role in the design and implementation of research projects, since they are far more attuned to local social and political expectations, risks, and conditions than outsiders. However, rarely are such partners acknowledged beyond a footnote in the published research output, even though their participation was essential for the project to be realized in the first place. Western researchers can easily rectify this issue by giving greater credit to local research partners who take risks and possess invaluable expertise.

To minimize risks to our respondents and partners, and to maximize the benefits for science, we worked closely with our partners in the field and studiously researched the region of interest. We found that at least some of our respondents were curious about our research topic and eagerly offered their expertise and participation in the study, which we believe reflects the importance of insurgent violence in public life in Dagestan. Respondents were likely also pleased to have an opportunity to reflect on some of the pressing issues of their day-to-day lives, on which the authorities have largely ignored their viewpoints.

The Element has seven sections and proceeds as follows. Section 2 delves into a discussion of the Dagestani context as an example of a dangerous research environment, where direct questioning techniques would not be appropriate, safe, or effective. It outlines the logic of our case selection, which points to the need for using indirect experimental approaches while also exploring questions of comparability and generalizability. Section 3 articulates a theory that links civilian support for the insurgency and their exposure to violence. We explain why direct civilian victimization can turn into an effective tool of social control in irregular wars. When civilians cannot switch sides (between jihadis and pro-government forces) due to thick religious and ethnic loyalties, security concerns, and local economic dependencies that embed them into the warring silos and limit their agency, defection is effectively denied. The theory also expects the effect of exposure to violence on civilian support for the insurgency to depend upon its *source* (the insurgency or the counterinsurgency violence), as well as on the type (whether it is experienced *directly* or *indirectly*). Section 4 explains why we opted for endorsement experiments over several alternatives, which we also evaluate in terms of their advantages and disadvantages, both in general and as applied to this specific study. Section 5 outlines the design considerations and the endorsement experiments for the specific context. Section 6 examines the main empirical results and their broader implications. Section 7 summarizes the Element's main contributions and offers several suggestions for future directions in experimental research using unobtrusive questioning techniques to probe sensitive topics in dangerous settings, where some of the most exciting and significant research in the social sciences is yet to be done. Although our specific emphasis in this Element is on why and when civilians support insurgent groups during irregular wars, we hope that readers will see its utility for studying a wide range of similarly difficult to elicit attitudes about taboo topics in dangerous settings. These methods provide scholars with important tools that can simultaneously reduce sensitivity bias and provide a high degree of safety for respondents, enumerators, and researchers.

2 Danger in Dagestan

Throughout the 1990s, Dagestan was relatively and remarkably safe, particularly when compared to many other republics in the Russian North Caucasus region (Figure 1). However, diffusion of violence from the neighboring Chechnya, along with the creation and solidification of the Caucasus Emirate (Imarat Kavkaz) in the 2000s, led to the rise of religious extremists. It transformed Dagestan into a dangerous place and, later, into a hot spot of global jihad. Dagestan is a poor, diverse, and geographically isolated region of Russia, famous for its internationally renowned mixed martial arts fighters. During the conflict, Dagestani civilians could not flee, migrate, or hunker down in safety – their choices were tremendously limited. Three factors, which we elaborate upon in this section and the next, shed light on why civilian options were so restricted: (1) sticky religious and ethnic identities; (2) economic dependence and welfare provision tied to clan-based communal life; and (3) security threats both from the insurgents and the government.

Since the late 2000s, Dagestan has become the primary location of Islamic insurgent violence in the Caucasus. While the causes are complex, the conflict has been driven largely by local factors (Campana and Ratelle 2014; Ratelle and Souleimanov 2017; Rozanova and Yarlykapov 2014; Sagramoso 2012).[9] Like many other republics in the region, Dagestan is underserviced by the central authorities in Moscow, in terms of both public infrastructure and personal

---

[9] These include corruption and clan competition for local resources, human rights abuses, religious repression, economic decline, and the spillover effects of the Chechen conflicts.

Figure 1 Dagestan and surrounding territories
Note: Shapefiles available for download at https://gadm.org/data.html.
Source: compiled by authors from open-source shapefiles.

security. Addressing economic grievances and overcoming cleavages among the republic's main ethnic groups have been the main challenges for Dagestan's political system. Similar difficulties prevail inside insurgent and religious groups, where ethnic and clan-based identities have often conflicted with the need for a common identity among the fighters. Physical, economic, and social protection of civilians during the conflict was provided in the silos of the warring parties. When the conflict escalated, the embedded nature of civilian life in local networks led to a situation where "defection was denied," as Dagestanis belonged either to the jihadi or to the pro-government camp.

One of the main defining features of Dagestani society is its ethnic and religious diversity. It is an extraordinarily complex multiethnic polity, with fourteen major ethnic groups and more than thirty local languages. Despite this diversity, not to mention the economic deprivation, Dagestan was relatively quiet throughout much of the 1990s, following the collapse of the Soviet Union. Much of this stability (especially compared to neighboring Chechnya at this time) was attributed to the consociational system of governance that provides representation and rotating power explicitly based on ethnicity for Avars, Dargins, Laks, Kumyks, and other less numerous ethnicities (Kisriev 2007; Ware and Kisriev 2001, 2009, 2010).

Against the backdrop of Dagestan's highly ethnically fractionalized society, ethnicity serves as the principal source of self-identification, with its relevance stretching well beyond established kinship ties. In their quotidian lives, individuals place enormous importance on ethnicity in general, and on ethnic solidarity in particular: marriage, communal life, employment, and politics all revolve around the notion of ethnicity-centered in-group solidarity (Tsapieva and Muslimov 2000). In Dagestan, the *umma* (the one Islamic nation), religious, ethnic, and *tukhum* (clan and clan groupings) loyalties are intertwined (Collombier and Roy 2018). In short, ethnicity has retained its significance, even among regional jihadi groups, who profess allegiance to a broader superordinate Salafi identity (Hahn 2011). Some *jamaats* are dominated by Avars and others by Kumyks, Laks, Dargins, and Lezgins, whereas other *jamaats* are ethnically mixed.

Religious diversity maps onto the insurgency as Salafism is the main driver of jihadism in Dagestan. A clan-based society, multiple identities and economic dependence have often hindered collective action. Those who advocate Salafism consider themselves believers in the unity of G-d (*muwahhidun*), and refuse to acknowledge any other source of identity – for example, ethnicity, class, tribe, race – than their religious identity as part of the global *umma* (the community of fellow Muslim believers).

Fighting against unbelief and sin (*kufr* and *haram*) has the potential to unite ethnicities and overcome clan loyalties, but the reality is more complex, since Dagestan's rural jihadi groups largely operate on a territorial-clan (*tukhum*) basis.[10] Communal life embedded in territorial clans reinforces local dependence, limits exit options, and checks defection. Given the salience of *tukhum*-based kinship in the republic's rural areas, authorities and law enforcement are often manned by the members of the same family (or clan) as the members of locally operating jihadi groups.[11] Therefore, physical safety is tied to local networks as well, for authorities provide protection selectively, based in part on kinship networks. Defection from kinship networks thus also directly endangers civilian safety, especially during a violent conflict.

Ethnic favoritism (*asabiyya*) is a widely recognized problem in multiethnic Dagestan (Ware and Kisriev 2001), and it has also pervaded the republic's jihadi groups, with members of disadvantaged ethnic groups expressing grievances

---

[10] This holds specifically for (ethnically homogenous) jihadi groups operating in rural areas, while jihadi groups operating in urban centers are usually ethnically mixed (see Souleimanov 2018a).

[11] Interview with Professor Akhmet Yarlykapov of the Moscow State Institute of International Relations, January 30, 2015. Akhmet Yarlykapov observed that "virtually everybody is someone's relative in the rural areas, so those who went to the woods [joined *jamaats*] are not eager to liquidate their relatives in the local administration and police - or *haram* attacks. The instances of killing relatives [. . .] became notorious just because they were so rare."

over discriminatory, un-Islamic practices. Ethnic-based clientelism is a form of economic and social dependence on patrons, which reduces generalized trust and universalism based on long-term horizons (Bustikova and Corduneanu-Huci 2017) and promotes parochial local identities. It is widely acknowledged that it induces ethnic loyalty and empowers local leaders. In 2010, an Islamic judge of Dagestan's largest *jamaat* Shariat even issued an internal *fatwa* calling for the leader of a minor *jamaat* operating in the Khasavyurt area to abandon ethnic favoritism or leave the jihad entirely (Souleimanov 2018b). In short, ethnic bonds in ethnically mixed *jamaats* are a serious issue that the leaders must tackle to succeed. Although the interlocking identities in Dagestan are complex, civilians live in relatively rigid and highly localized clan-based ethnic networks that limit their room for defection.

2.1 Introducing the Insurgency

Dagestan is a dangerous place today, and it was unsafe when we conducted this study in 2015. Relatively peaceful throughout much of the 1990s (for reasons discussed in Derlugian 1999; Holland and O'Loughlin 2010; Kisriev 2007; and Ware et al. 2003), insurgent violence in Dagestan began to rise around the same time that it declined in Chechnya (Lyall 2009; Souleimanov and Siroky 2016). In 2007 in Chechnya, local rebel leader Doku Umarov proclaimed the indigenous Islamic rebel organization, the Caucasus Emirate. The declaration marked a decisive shift from the Chechen nationalist goal of creating independent Chechnya to a pan-Caucasian goal of establishing an Islamic state (Toft and Zhukov 2015).[12] Dagestan played a key role early on in the Caucasus Emirate.[13]

Violence peaked around 2011 in Dagestan (Kolosov and Sebentcov 2014; Schaefer 2010; Souleimanov 2011; Toft and Zhukov 2015; Zurcher 2007). Soon after Umarov's death in 2013, and due to the growing weight of Dagestan and diminishing importance of Chechnya in the insurgency, ethnic Dagestanis assumed leadership in the organization. Several active jihadi groups – working under the umbrella of the Caucasus Emirate and ISIS – coexisted in Dagestan at least from the end of 2014 until late 2015.[14] Aliaskhab Kebekov, the first

---

[12] For a review of ethnonationalist secession and self-determination movements, see Siroky and Abbasov 2021.

[13] For example, the head of the mono-ethnic rural Gubden *Jamaat*, Ibrahimhalil Daudov, was considered one of the leaders of Dagestani jihadism. A "founding co-father" of the jihadist "Caucasus Emirate" across the North Caucasus in 2007, he became the head of the all-Dagestani "*Jamaat* Shariat" in 2010. The leader of the mono-ethnic Levashinskiy *jamaat*, Rappani Khalilov, was also considered an important jihadi ideologue, and attracted religiously motivated recruits. See Siroky et al. 2021.

[14] Including the *Jamaat* Shariat, the Khasavyurskiy *Jamaat*, the Shamilkalinskiy *Jamaat*, the Nogaiskiy *Jamaat*, the Gubdenskiy *Jamaat*, the Buynakskiy *Jamaat*, and the Southern (Derbentskiy) *Jamaat*.

Dagestani to lead the Caucasus Emirate, was killed in April 2015, and was succeeded by another Dagestani, Magomed Suleymanov, who was killed in August of the same year. Following these and other fatalities, the Caucasus Emirate became merely a shadow of its former self by the end of the year.[15]

From 2010 to the summer of 2015, when the survey in this study was carried out, roughly 400 civilians were killed, in a territory with less than three million people, and several thousands of Dagestanis were exposed to violence (Figure 2).[16] Threats and violence against civilians in Dagestan came in a variety of forms, including assassinations, extra-legal executions, extortions, and unlawful arrests, amongst others.[17] Islamist insurgents sometimes killed civilians for ideological reasons. For example, they targeted sellers of alcohol for breaking Islamic norms and engaging in *haram* (forbidden) practices, as well as targeting traditional healers for practicing "witchcraft" (Siroky et al. 2021). Another widespread practice was extorting funds from local businesses.[18]

In many irregular wars, civilians often lack viable options for remaining neutral (Kalyvas and Kocher 2007) or switching sides. Defection is discouraged. In Dagestan, this was largely the case at the time of the survey, and remains so at the time of writing. Compartmentalization of the warring camps follows cleavages organized in the clan-based system, which serves as a social base that has been exploited by both sides. Many people found (and still find) themselves at risk of counterinsurgency abuses and violence, which have included "prophylactic" arrests, kidnappings, torture, and killings. A respected Russian human rights organization, "Memorial," estimated that government agencies kidnapped at least eighteen people in Dagestan in 2009 alone, the majority of whom were later found dead or declared as

---

[15] The transition temporarily boosted violence in the region. In 2016, as compared to 2015, there was a spike of violence in Dagestan. However, the casualties have since dwindled (see www .kavkaz-uzel.eu/articles/317689/). At the peak in 2010–2011, the casualties in Dagestan, including dead and wounded individuals, reached 1705 (2010) and 1375 (2011).

[16] The statistics for victims of violence in the North Caucasus in 2011–2019 by *Kavkazskiy Uzel*, www.kavkaz-uzel.eu/articles/statistika_jertv_2010_2015.html.

[17] In Dagestan, civilians distinguish between the motivations and powers at the regional and the national levels. For instance, Dagestani authorities outlawed "wahabism," whereas national authorities did not. This antagonized the support base of the rebels and contributed to the creation of sectarian tensions between Sufis and Salafis.

[18] While the traditional teaching in Dagestan was Sufism, the insurgency adopted Salafism, which has spread conflict among Muslim Caucasians, leading to a number of notorious murders, including the mufti of Dagestan, Said Afandi, who was killed by a female suicide bomber, posing as a pilgrim in his home. The bomber was an ethnic Russian convert to Islam. Even though the insurgents did not officially claim responsibility for the attack, the profile of bomber suggests that "the Forest Brothers" sent her as a *shahida* (female martyr). See www.kavkaz-uzel.eu/articles/211915/.

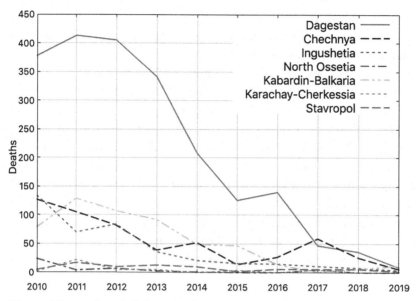

Figure 2 Dynamics of violence in the North Caucasus over time, 2010–2019
Source: *Compiled by authors. The statistics of victims of violence in the North Caucasus in 2010–2019 by Kavkazskiy Uzel, Available at* www.kavkaz-uzel.eu/articles/statistika_jertv_2010_2015.html.

"disappeared."[19] The number of kidnapped individuals in the territory peaked at twenty-nine in 2011.[20]

At the time of our survey in 2015, the rebels were taking many more losses than the counterinsurgency forces, and the insurgency was on the run, but there was still a non-negligible amount of rebel violence against civilians. While it is often hard to conduct such research at the height of violence for logistical reasons, we felt it was important to do it as soon as it was feasible so that the memory of recent violence was fresh in mind, rendering questions about exposure to violence crisper in the respondents' recollections (Bar-Anan et al. 2006; Liberman et al. 2002).

In irregular wars, it is sometimes – maybe more often than not – hard to determine whether the individuals targeted by the counterinsurgency were innocent civilians or insurgents, due to both the sparse information environment and the incentives for opposing sides to misrepresent. For example, in 2016, after killing two brothers, Nabi and Gasangusein Gasanguseinov, the government

---

[19] Source: https://memohrc.org/sites/all/themes/memo/templates/pdf.php?pdf=/uploads/files/451.pdf.
[20] Source: https://memohrc.org/sites/all/themes/memo/templates/pdf.php?pdf=/uploads/files/649.pdf.

declared both of them to be militants.[21] Later, however, the government recognized that the brothers were killed by mistake and closed the criminal case against them, while opening another one to probe their killing (though no officials have been prosecuted for the crime to date). Sometimes entire villages were subject to mass punishment at the hands of the counterinsurgency (e.g., the Dagestani village of Gimry).[22] After repeatedly failing to root out the insurgency in this one village through indiscriminate violence, which entailed many civilian causalities, the counterinsurgency forced the villagers to relocate to a new settlement – Vremenny (Russian for "Temporary") – where the police continued its mop-up operations. In many villages across Dagestan, counterinsurgency operations were a daily occurrence: some forces would seal the village perimeter, while others in armored vehicles would destroy homes and suspects inside them using thermobaric weaponry.

The Russian government has one of the most capable militaries in the world and is one of the leading nations in military spending.[23] A characteristic manifestation of this power asymmetry was territorial control: the insurgents did not reliably control any part of Dagestan despite its extremely rough terrain with mountains and forests (Siroky and Dzutsev 2015).[24] This distinguishes it from cases where the insurgency is arguably stronger than the incumbents, such as Afghanistan.[25] As a result of this asymmetry, the counterinsurgency had little incentive to negotiate with the rebels, and civilians were largely unwilling (and unable) to defect.[26] The counterinsurgency forces imposed heavy penalties on Dagestanis whom they considered to have any ties to insurgency.

A government commission for the adaptation and reintegration of rebels to civilian life was created in Dagestan, but its impact remained miniscule. The governmental body had no power to exonerate anybody. For example, for two years in 2011–2012, the commission said forty-six people came to ask for assistance. More than half of them ended up in prison.[27] At least one of the

---

[21] After their home village rose in protest against the government cover up, a criminal investigation was launched into the killing. Source: www.eng.kavkaz-uzel.eu/articles/42564/.

[22] Gimry is also famous in Dagestan for being the homeland of national heroes, who used to fight Russians in the nineteenth century – imam Shamil and imam Gazimagomed.

[23] See SIPRI at www.sipri.org/databases/milex.

[24] With the sole exception of several months in 1999, particularly at night.

[25] On Russia's approach to interventions, compared to the West and in relation to it, see Allison 2013.

[26] In 2015, the cost of switching to the rebel side was much higher than switching to the government side. Even the rebel leaders could not usually last more than several months, as they were usually killed in battle. For ordinary rebels, survival was arguably even more dangerous, so defection was, if anything, only a one-way valve to join the rebels.

[27] Timur Isaev and Karina Gadzhieva. "In Dagestan the Commission on Adaptation of Fighters Considered 46 Applications in Two Years," *Kavkazsky Uzel*, November 2, 2012, www.kavkaz-uzel.eu/articles/215088/

members of the commission stated that not a single actual rebel addressed the commission directly. Instead, it was usually civilians with some connection to the rebels that came to ask to clear them.[28] Even that appeared to be a difficult task. Out of the thousands of rebels and civilians involved (in one way or another) with the insurgency in Dagestan, only a handful turned themselves in to the commission. Experts said that the legal foundations of the commission were shaky, and few people could trust a commission without powers to grant amnesty that had a record of putting petitioners for forgiveness behind bars. Reports frequently emerged that government forces did not take prisoners during special operations, and that some alleged militants and sometimes civilians were found dead after police arrests or kidnappings.[29] Harsh government tactics evidently did not facilitate the defection of active rebels – quite the contrary, it hardened positions.

Torture, kidnappings, and extrajudicial killings were common counterinsurgency practices.[30] All civilians who at any point provided any assistance to the rebel side could be subject to prosecution.[31] One of the only options to civilians, particularly to Salafis, who did not wish to side with the pro-Russian armed actors was to flee Dagestan and Russia altogether (Barter 2017), which Dagestanis did in large numbers, mainly to the Middle East to join IS's supporters in Iraq and Syria between 2014–2017 toward the end of the conflict in Dagestan. No exact numbers are known, but most estimates put the number of radical Muslim Dagestanis who emigrated to Syria and Iraq at several thousand.[32] Unlike the situation in Afghanistan, where the Taliban could punish civilians who supported ISAF, Dagestani insurgents' ability to inflict pain on civilians who supported counterinsurgency (at the time of our survey) was quite limited. Compared to the Taliban, the insurgency in Dagestan had no territorial

---

[28] Akhmednabi Akhmednabiev. "Kebedov: In Dagestan not a Single Real Militant has Passed Through the Commission on Adaptation," *Kavazsky Uzel*, December 11, 2011, www.kavkaz-uzel.eu/articles/197442/. For instance, people who provided food or shelter, but did not fight. The commission sought to mediate between civilians and police but had no power to grant amnesty.

[29] Rasul Magomedov. "Chechen SC Refuses to Rehabilitate Dagestani Residents Killed by Law Enforcers," *Kavkazsky Uzel*, March 10, 2020. www.eng.kavkaz-uzel.eu/articles/50253/.

[30] See, for example, "Dagestan: Extrajudicial Executions Continue," *Human Rights Center Memorial*, February 21, 2012, https://memohrc.org/ru/news/dagestan-vnesudebnye-kazni-prodolzhayutsya; "Invisible War: Russia's Abusive Response to the Dagestan Insurgency," *Human Rights Watch*, June 18, 2015, www.hrw.org/report/2015/06/18/invisible-war/russias-abusive-response-dagestan-insurgency.

[31] Article 201.1 of the Russian Criminal Code envisages five years to life imprisonment for people providing any assistance to insurgents.

[32] In January 2017, the Dagestani Interior Ministry estimated the number of Dagestanis fighting for ISIS in Syria at 1,200 militants. This number did not include family members who often joined the men. "The Ministry of Internal Affairs Counted Over a Thousand Dagestanis in the Ranks of IS in Syria," *Kavkazsky Uzel* www.kavkaz-uzel.eu/articles/296890/.

control over any district, even though they continued to exercise a degree of control over civilians. This raises important questions and issues related to domain knowledge and generalizability.

2.2 Domain Knowledge and Generalizability

Is Dagestan's jihadi rebellion unique? Since irregular wars without foreign occupying forces (sometimes called "homegrown rebellions") are far more common than those with major power interventions, Afghanistan and Iraq are exceptional cases in that they involved direct Western participation on the ground. On this count, Dagestan is a more typical case, yet it also possesses some particularities that are important to keep in mind when seeking to understand how civilians perceive the conflict and how respondents are likely to react to a survey on it.

Three features strike us as crucial for our study, and, we think, with appropriate adjustment for other studies on similar subjects. The first factor is the cultural affinity between the insurgency, the civilian population, and the counterinsurgency that stems from the territorial clan-based society. This is crucial for understanding the potential allegiances. The second factor is a large power asymmetry between the fighting sides, which is critical for understanding the strategies and constraints of all actors and side-switching options for civilians: defections are rare. The third factor concerns the time horizons of the insurgents, which is essential for understanding their priorities and their relationship with civilians.

Unlike some insurgencies, where the members are ethnically, religiously, linguistically, and otherwise distinct from the counterinsurgency forces, Dagestan represents a situation in which the civilians, insurgents, and counterinsurgents are all culturally proximate.[33] Despite the fact that Dagestan is the most ethnically diverse region in the Russian Federation, the overall ethnic makeup of the civilian population, the insurgency, and the counterinsurgency is very much alike. Compared to ISAF in Afghanistan, for example, the cultural distance between the localized counterinsurgency forces and the civilian population in Dagestan is very small.

Since Russia was seeking to restore order in a restive region of its own country and locals had been exposed to the Russian language and culture for generations, pro-Russian forces were not technically an occupying force in Dagestan. The warring parties shared generations of common socialization and a mutual language. Relatedly – and even more central, we think – a large

---

[33] There is some overlap between religious cleavages and the two sides: the (Salafi) minority is associated with the rebels and the (Sufi) majority is affiliated with the counterinsurgency.

part of the counterinsurgency was made up of ethnic Dagestanis themselves. This cultural proximity (or distance) is often an important element in really understanding what it means to "support" one or the other of the fighting sides in an irregular war.

Second, the power asymmetry between the insurgency and the counterinsurgency in Dagestan was considerable, and probably larger than in most conflicts (Balcells and Kalyvas 2014).[34] Compared to Afghanistan, for example, where the Taliban was much stronger than the local Afghan forces and could hold its own even against Western ISAF forces, the Caucasus Emirate in Dagestan, especially in 2015, was much weaker than the counterinsurgency forces. As an indicator, the rebels in Dagestan lacked territorial control over almost all areas with civilian populations, where the counterinsurgency had a clear advantage. While many insurgencies hold some territory, for at least some period of time, the Caucasus Emirate was largely without civilian territory for the duration of its existence.[35] However, the insurgency exercised control over villagers and civilians loyal to them.

Third, there is a crucial temporal aspect to all surveys that speaks to their ability to generalize, and our study is no exception. Since survey experiments occur at specific moments in time, the contemporaneous temporal features shape how the respondents experience the conflict and understand the questions asked of them. It also constrains how far into the future the results are likely to be valid. At the time of the survey, the insurgency was much weaker than it had been only a few years earlier. Some allegiances in Dagestan were transitioning toward Islamic State, but on the whole the insurgency remained a local affair. As a result, competing rebel factions were primarily targeting their support base, consistent with the logic of "disorder" under rebel rule when factions with short time horizons fight for influence (Arjona 2016).

As we argue in Section 3, the support base of the rebels in this context was much more likely to be targeted by insurgents seeking to establish control over "their" civilians and to whip them into compliance. Consequently, given limited options to defect to the pro-government side, we expect civilians to "double down" and to increase their support in response to direct victimization by the insurgents.

---

[34] Balcells and Kalyvas (2014, p. 1393) note that irregular wars are endogenous to the relative weakness of rebels compared to the government.

[35] According to one source, roughly two-thirds of all rebel groups from 1946–2011 did not possess any territorial control, and so the insurgency in Dagestan is not at all unique in this regard. Source: http://ksgleditsch.com/eacd.html.

Although the insurgency was relatively weak, it nonetheless continued to hold ideological appeal for some civilians. Moreover, those who had already clearly sided with the rebels had either left for Syria and Iraq or had little choice but stick with them, regardless of their ideological appeal, since switching was very costly. By contrast, civilians who experienced direct victimization at the hands of the counterinsurgency already belonged to the anti-insurgency camp in many cases, and switching to the insurgency was more costly to them than staying where they were. Consequently, rather than falling into the arms of the insurgency, as in Afghanistan, civilians in Dagestan expressed even less support for the insurgency after government forces victimized them.

These three features – rebel time horizons, power asymmetry, and cultural proximity – are not unique to Dagestan. For other studies, we think that these factors – their presence, absence, and extent – may influence the way respondents answer questions and how we as researchers should think about the interpretation of the results when conducting endorsement experiments, or any other surveys or inquiries. Since we were interested in exploring a typical case, we chose a violent region with a civil conflict with a domestic counterinsurgency force (like the Russian and pro-Russian forces in Dagestan), and without a foreign counterinsurgency (like NATO or ISAF). The study also had to be feasible, so within this framework we selected a place that was not so insulated as to render surveying it impossible (e.g., Chechnya). We ultimately chose Dagestan over Chechnya due to the viability of implementing a survey experiment on this (or any sensitive) topic, and also because it had a more robust insurgency at this time than did Chechnya. In neighboring Chechnya, the political regime at the time (and, as of our writing, still) was so rigid that running a survey of this kind and on these topics was not thought feasible by our local collaborators when we were developing the research plan. The regional government in Dagestan had a looser grip on the locals and did not block the survey implementation. At the time of the survey, Dagestan was also the most violent place in the Russian North Caucasus (see Figure 3), in addition to being the largest republic, and therefore afforded the best opportunity to examine the substantive issues we wanted to explore using experimental techniques.

Finally, we were looking for a case that was not "identical" to previous studies, but was still sufficiently typical to facilitate comparison, to explore the scope conditions, and to assess generalizability (Gerring and Cojocaru 2016, p. 399; Seawright 2016, pp. 75, 85–92). While all irregular wars share some commonalities, further replications, extensions, and comparisons in different contexts are always necessary to reveal the extent to which the Dagestani (Afghani, or any other) experience is generalizable. Shadish, Cook, and Campbell (2002, p. 19) define two types of generalization. The first is

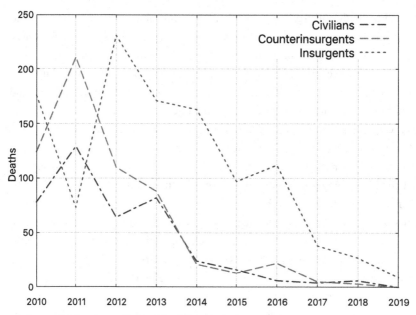

Figure 3 Number of killed individuals in insurgent and counterinsurgent
violence in Dagestan in 2010–2019

Source: *Compilations of authors. The statistics of victims of violence in the North Caucasus in 2010–2019 by Kavkazskiy Uzel, Available at www.kavkaz-uzel.eu/articles/ statistika_jertv_2010_2015.html.*

a generalization to "units, treatments, variables and settings not directly observed," and the second is to the "domain about which the questions are asked." Applied to this study, these two concerns about generalizability imply: 1) issues that arise with the construct validity of the items probed in the questionnaire and the representativeness of the sample and 2) concerns about the limited geographic nature of any study and the extent to which the results will apply to other settings.

Combining random sampling with random assignment to indirect questioning ensures that the results are representative of Dagestan. Endorsement experiments address problems with evasive responses that can lead to misleading conclusions. However, to ascertain construct validity for our target concept – "support for insurgents" – one needs to integrate qualitative, contextual knowledge and research. The integration of qualitative research and domain knowledge with experimental research is crucial for the advancement of experimental research in the social sciences. In this spirit, we scoured specialized media outlets and consulted with local experts to ensure a strong correspondence between the concept and the measurements.

We focused our efforts on two main areas: 1) how to determine the most neutral name for the insurgency, and 2) how to select and design the specific policies to be used for the experiments. We discuss these further in Section 4. We sought to incorporate this research about Dagestan into the survey design in a meaningful manner, ensuring that the questions, terminology, and policies represent to the respondents the actual concepts and events we intended. Finally, after the research is complete, deep contextual knowledge of the region and the conflict is vital for interpreting the results, and in order to extract substantive meaning.

The Dagestani case brings the study of civilian attitudes toward insurgencies and militant groups to a new region with a unique mix of actors, ideologies, cleavages, and histories, and to an extremely complex ethnolinguistic setting. Only by extending our knowledge of this phenomenon to new types of irregular wars and new geographic regions of the world can we hope to construct, by collective efforts, a solid foundation for general knowledge. Dagestan is distinct from Afghanistan in being an example of a homegrown rebellion against a domestic government's counterinsurgency. It is also different from Pakistan, due to the much stronger central state, less permeable borders, and a communist and command-economy legacy. The literature has thus far focused on cases where counterinsurgency is either waged by a foreign occupying force (ISAF or NATO), and cases where the counterinsurgency force is a potent non-democratic *domestic* government with large numbers of local coethnic members have been largely overlooked in experimental studies. Yet this is arguably a much more typical scenario, since irregular wars without major foreign-power occupying forces have been more common in modern history.

The scope conditions that are satisfied in Dagestan are certainly not universal – indeed, no conflict zone can make that claim – but many of its features are quite typical, and we believe they travel quite broadly to other homegrown insurgencies. To that extent, the results presented and discussed here could apply to many countries and conflicts in different regions around the world: the Dagestani insurgency can provide general lessons for understanding the relationship between civilians, violence, and support for insurgency during irregular wars elsewhere. When researchers seek to probe civilian attitudes toward rebels during any active insurgency, direct questioning is often not a reasonable option because of safety, ethics, and/or efficacy.

We have provided some crucial context for this study, albeit still only a small portion of the historical and current setting. We have also elucidated some of the most critical reasons for selecting Dagestan to study civilian support for insurgency and and the generalizability of the case. The next section introduces our theory that rests on the premise that civilian "defection is denied" and derives several testable hypotheses.

3 Theory: Defection Denied

"For years, counterinsurgency operations were a daily routine in Dagestan. Ordinarily, the counterinsurgency would use armored vehicles, thermobaric weapons, and other equipment as needed. The best trained government forces (often those associated with the Russian federal agencies) would confront the militants, while the local police forces would guard the perimeter of the operation. Insurgents were usually armed with machine guns, rifles, and grenades. Once the counterinsurgency detected suspects, the area would be surrounded, and homes destroyed with everyone inside them. Sometimes, civilians managed to negotiate their surrender – sometimes, they did not.

On April 19, 2015, the government forces sealed off an area in the settlement of Gerei-Avlak in the suburbs of the city of Buinaksk in Dagestan. The government suspected that several leaders of the Islamist insurgency movement, the Caucasus Emirate, were inside one of the private homes. . . . the counterinsurgency was in luck when they managed to raid a home with the then leader of the Caucasus Emirate Aliaskhab Kebekov inside. After a brief negotiation, the government forces allowed two children and a couple who owned the house to come out and surrender. Next, the storm ensued, which killed five people, including three rebels and two women, the rebels' wives."[36]

Why do civilians support rebels in irregular wars? We argue that civilian support for militant groups stems from their embeddedness in communal life and dependence on local power structures, and in this case on clan ties. When violence erupted, Dagestani civilians found themselves in one of the warring camps, with limited options to switch sides. "Defection was denied" by both the jihadis and the pro-governmental forces. Civilian compliance was re-enforced not only via economic dependence, derived from ethnic favoritism and *tukhum* loyalties, but also through violence. As a result, civilian victimization did not engender resistance but instead solidified loyalty, dependence, and obedience. Civilian abuse is of course problematic, even in wartime, but it does appear to be an effective strategy for the rebels and pro-governmental forces to ensure compliance in the conflict.

Theorists and practitioners of irregular war and counterinsurgency have long recognized that domestic conflicts are shaped by the ability of each side to win over civilian support, or at least to enforce civilian acquiescence (Kilcullen 2009; Trinquier 2006; US Army 2007). In irregular wars, civilian support can supply or deny shelter, material aid, and information. Although practitioners

---

[36] "Dagestan: Chronicles of Terror 1996–2020," April 22, 2021, *Kavkazsky Uzel*, www.kavkaz-uzel.eu/articles/73122/ [authors' translation from several articles].

agree that civilians are central actors in many civil wars, a large part of the scholarly literature ignores civilians altogether; and, when they are included, the main focus has been on civilians as targets, seeking to explain variation in their victimization by rebel and counterinsurgency attacks (Balcells 2010; Downes 2008; Salehyan, Siroky, and Wood 2014; Weinstein 2007; Wood 2003).

While this is an important aspect of civilians' experience during irregular wars and worthy of investigation, more recent literature has begun to disaggregate what civilians can and cannot do, and what support actually means, in the midst of an irregular war (Arjona 2016, 2017; Barter 2017; Hirose, Imai, and Lyall 2017; Kaplan 2017; Parkinson 2013). When civilians are victimized, there is a need to examine, in different contexts, how disparate sources and forms of exposure to violence influence civilian attitudes.[37] Advancing our understanding of civilian attitudes requires gaining access to non-combatants during civil wars and obtaining reliable answers to dangerous lines of inquiry without putting the respondents, enumerators, or analysts at risk.

Several recent micro-level studies have investigated the determinants of civilian support for militancy and insurgency using rigorous research designs. The focus has thus far been on three countries (Afghanistan, Iraq, and Pakistan) and on a region with extensive US military involvement (e.g., Blair et al. 2013; Bullock, Imai, and Shapiro 2011; Fair and Shepherd 2006; Lyall, Blair, and Imai 2013; Shapiro and Fair 2009).[38] Lyall, Blair, and Imai (2013), for instance, published a seminal study of civilian support for the Taliban and ISAF during the war in Afghanistan that serves as an exemplar in the field and a model for this study in particular. It explores the effects of in-group and out-group identities on support for the Taliban and ISAF, and finds a strong "home team" advantage for the Taliban. Bullock, Imai, and Shapiro (2011) also use endorsement experiments to measure support for militant groups in Pakistan.

These innovative studies have provided new, sometimes counterintuitive, insights into what shapes civilian support in irregular wars, particularly in the aforementioned countries. This places our understanding of the role of civilians on much firmer empirical ground on the basis of micro-level data and experimental designs. Building upon this research program, we bring it to a new context to study the local insurgency in Dagestan, Russia. This allows us to assess some relationships between militant support and exposure to violence in

---

[37] Prior research on civilian behavior has emphasized territorial control (e.g., Kalyvas 2006; Kalyvas and Kocher 2007), competitive goods delivery (e.g., Berman et al. 2011; Crost, Felter and Johnston 2014), and violence against civilians (e.g., Condra and Shapiro. 2012; Kocher et al. 2011; Lyall et al. 2013).

[38] Other studies that have examined civilians in irregular wars using ethnographic or historical methods have focused on weak states, mostly in Asia, Africa, and Latin America, whereas Russia is a substantially stronger state, in more ways than one.

a setting with Russian, as opposed to American, involvement, and in a conflict and context that are quite distinct from existing studies, yet quite common in irregular wars that pitch rebels against their own governments.

How can we study civilian support for the insurgency, and assess the factors theorized to correlate with support in irregular wars, while minimizing risk, acquiring reliable responses, and protecting those involved? The framework utilized here focuses on measuring the latent level of support for the insurgency, using indirect questioning techniques, and then examining the effects of two factors – *the type of exposure* (direct violence or hearsay) to violence and *the source* (who did it) of that violence – on the latent level of civilian support for the insurgency, using a Bayesian measurement model.

This approach builds on previous studies that have emphasized the role of violence in the formation of civilian attitudes (Blair et al. 2013; Bullock, Imai, and Shapiro 2011; Lyall, Blair, and Imai 2013).[39] We also build on the distinction between the effects of direct exposure to violence (experienced firsthand by the respondent or his/her family, thus based on fact) and the effects of indirect exposure to violence (heard about happening to someone else in the area, based on perception, rumor or hearsay). This is what we mean by the "type" of exposure to violence: direct or indirect. We also emphasize the "source" of the violence, which means whether it comes from the insurgency or from the counterinsurgency. After theorizing how these different types of exposure and sources of violence influence civil support for the insurgency, we propose and assess six specific hypotheses, which we discuss in more detail in Section 3.1. In the course of doing this, we also explain why direct civilian victimization by rebels is an effective tool of social control in irregular wars.

3.1 Civilians as "Hostages"

Civilian life in Dagestan is characterized by embeddedness in territorially based clan networks and ethnic favoritism. This implies that, even in times of peace, civilians rely on local ties for jobs, welfare, and physical safety. This dependence is amplified by sticky ethnic identities that are a prerequisite for access to economic resources.[40] Civilians are bound to depend on local information networks and communities. When the rebellion started, the government forces and the insurgents doubled down on their control of civilians by cutting off their exit options and opportunities to defect. Civilians were locked into the two

---

[39] Rozenas and Zhukov (2019) show how authoritarian states can use repression to enforce loyalty among civilians.

[40] On the linkage between ethnicity and political allegiances, see Bustikova (2019).

opposing camps and violence became a form of social control to enforce compliance.

Unfortunately, competition between rebel groups escalated civilian abuse even further. We know from some studies (e.g., Ibragimov and Matsuzato 2014) and from our knowledge of the situation on the ground that rebels in Dagestan were most likely to interact with (and sometimes to victimize) their support base (the rebel "segment") in order to confirm and, if needed, re-establish control. As Arjona (2016) argues, when different rebel factions fight for the support of civilians, the rebel groups' time horizons shorten because they value the immediate outcome of survival over longer-term goals such as establishing a sustainable enduring relationship with civilians. Arjona (2016, p.3) convincingly demonstrates the influence of rebel time horizons on the development of distinct types of social orders underwritten by rebels: a comprehensive local governance ("rebelocracy"), a form of lesser control ("aliocracy"), or failure to form any type of social contract ("disorder").

Such infighting can result in the breakdown of the social order that had existed under rebel rule when communal compliance was enforced via non-violent means. When this happens, supporters of the insurgency will be more exposed to direct violence from the rebels than will non-supporters, as competing insurgency leaders try to (re-)establish the system of monitoring and sanctioning (Hechter 1988), and in the process engage in some selective violence against their support base to demonstrate their capacities and shore up loyalty. Despite being targeted by rebels, these adherents of the insurgency will, on average, continue to express support for them, since they prefer the rebel side compared to the government, but also crucially because they cannot easily defect to the government side without severe repercussions – both moral and material.

Civilians who interact directly (often as a result of being victimized or caught in a crime) with the counterinsurgency are much less likely to be in the rebel camp. Crucially, most if not all of them would presumably prefer to be subject to secular justice rather than harsh Islamic justice. Moreover, such individuals are likely to have been involved in noninsurgency-related activities, such as drunk-driving, illegal street trade, or other illicit or hazardous activities that would attract the attention of the police. Although they may not be fond of the counterinsurgency, they are surely better off siding with them than with the rebels, and thus rationally side with the counterinsurgency as the lesser of two evils.

In the absence of credible and secure ways to switch sides, civilian identities (pro- and anti-insurgency) harden over time. This is what happened in Dagestan, which has experienced ongoing conflict since the late 1990s. A similar logic applies to the civilians "captive" to the Islamists. Being directly targeted by the insurgents makes civilians more likely to support the insurgency, particularly because switching sides, protesting, and joining the pro-Russian population are not viable options.

Some literature has highlighted how the compartmentalization of violence among rebel networks can influence civilian attitudes and behaviors (Parkinson 2013). Civilians subjected to violence and denied the option to defect some-times develop Stockholm Syndrome, whereby "hostages" come to identify with their "captors." In Dagestan, the ties that bind civilians to their abusers are not only about the power to inflict harm, but also relate to their ideological prefer-ences, embeddedness in territorial networks, and economic dependence, which are more or less "symbiotic." Clan and ethnic ties, which link particular groups and tribes to certain more or less mono-ethnic *jamaats*, constrain the fluidity of the situation even in peace time. Pro-rebel civilians tend to be adherents of radical Islamic views, while pro-government civilians tend to be moderate Muslims or even absolutely secular. Switching from one side to the other requires more than adopting outward signs and taking fealties – it is usually a longer-term commitment, with moral and other strings attached. Defection is costly and is not encouraged.

In theory, civilians have a variety of options regarding how they interact with insurgencies, ranging from enlisting in the rebel organization to resisting it, and more passive options in between (Arjona 2016). Similar actions are, in prin-ciple, available to civilians with regard to the counterinsurgency too, especially if pro-government forces want to win over civilians. However, when the government side (the counterinsurgency) is so much stronger than the rebel side, and it already possesses much of the necessary knowledge about the local terrain and clan networks, it can more easily afford to neglect the "hearts and minds" of civilians, and even more so if it is a non-democratic regime (Hazelton 2017; Souleimanov, Siroky, and Krause 2021). This does not mean that civilians are not a factor in the government's calculations. Rather, it signifies that the government can afford to neglect the opinions and aspirations of part of the population under certain circumstances (i.e., a powerful and undemocratic state, acculturation of the target population, internal divisions in the target population).

Furthermore, civilians under the secular rule of pro-government forces may fear Sharia, which Islamic rebels would seek to implement as the law of the land if their power increased. These individuals have no incentives to switch sides; the current government may be corrupt and less than ideal in many ways, but some form of rebelocracy would in this case be disastrous for such individuals. Limited exit options (Hirschman 1970; Tiebout 1956) for leaving either the rebel "segment" or the government "segment" – and the inability to relocate within the country or to emigrate – can render civilians captives to their respective rulers.

Moreover, when the government imposes harsh penalties on civilians for supporting the rebels, and is capable of enforcing them, the options for civilians are further restricted. Once civilians ended up supporting the insurgency, the counterinsurgency effectively blocks their opportunities for defection by imposing severe penalties. These punishments are highly unpredictable in a non-democratic political environment, and therefore even more frightening.

Civilians who opted for the counterinsurgency-side face a dilemma of their own. Although they may be able to switch to the rebel side with slightly greater ease than pro-rebel individuals who might seek to join the counterinsurgency, joining the rebel side means no way back for them and a significant increase in the risk of being killed, compared to the odds of being killed among counter-insurgents and civilians (see Figure 3). It also entails subjecting themselves to strict Sharia law. In this setting, the result has been that two "segments" emerge in society: one containing supporters of the rebels and the other supporters of the government. The bargaining ranges for both groups thus exist only within each group's "segment," due to the extremely high costs for defecting from the rebel side to the government side or vice versa.[41]

This framework leads us to expect intimidation tactics, such as direct victimization, to be associated with increased support for the perpetrators who subjugate civilians. A relatively strong counterinsurgency, backed by a non-democratic government, will impose severe penalties on civilians for any cooperation with the rebels, while religious fundamentalists will enforce compliance among its base. Hence, we hypothesize that, all else equal:

(H1a) direct insurgent violence *increases* support for the insurgency

The conflict in Dagestan (and the wider North Caucasus region in Russia) has strong religious overtones, since the insurgency in Dagestan is dominated by adherents of Salafi teachings, which is known for its strict applications of Sharia, in particular *fikh* (the law of Islam). The insurgency is associated with radical Islamic views of Salafists, while the counterinsurgency is associated with moderate Sufis or secularists, the official representatives of Islam in Dagestan.[42] Both groups are Dagestanis and Muslims, but there are substantial ideological differences, which renders switching sides between them costly,

---

[41] Estimates for the relative sizes of these segments are notoriously unreliable.

[42] This clear division between radical Salafis and pliable Sufis is in itself a simplification of the complex reality of the religious landscape of Dagestan (Yarlykapov 2010), but it holds by and large, and especially at the time of our study.

both for Salafis who would wish to switch to the moderate side and for the moderates who would face a much stricter Islamic regime.

Implementation of Sharia in Dagestan is not a purely theoretical whim of Islamic theologians. Radical Islamists have attacked alcohol sellers, healers, and other businesses in the territory (Siroky et al. 2021). Sufi leaders, including the mufti of Dagestan, Sheikh Said Afandi, have been assassinated.[43] So, the threat of Islamic radicalism is today (and was in 2015, when the study was conducted) real for many Dagestanis.

The republic-level government outlawed "Wahhabism" (the term "Salafism" appears later) in September 1999.[44] Legislators passed the ban on Salafism soon after the central government in Moscow launched a military operation to wipe out an Islamist enclave in the western part of Dagestan in August 1999. The insurgents briefly acquired and held some territorial control over several villages in 1997–1999 (Yarlykapov 2010: p.140). After the massive incursion of Russian troops and the end of the war in neighboring Chechnya, the rebels in Dagestan never enjoyed territorial control during daylight over any part of the republic again.

In addition to insurgency-related violence, the government forces have also had to deal with many small-time infractions, such as traffic violations, theft, illegal street trade, etc. Since the rebels in Dagestan adhere to a strict view of Sharia, which is much harsher about punishing people for their transgressions than secular laws, people who have committed these misdemeanors and felonies will on average be substantially better off facing secular laws (enforced by the counterinsurgency) than facing extreme applications of *fikh* (from the insurgency). Also, certain social groups, and especially women, might find secular law more beneficial than the more discriminatory and restrictive Sharia law (Lazarev 2019).

As a result, rather than pushing civilians into the arms of the insurgents, unlike the results in a study of Afghanistan (Lyall et al. 2013), we predict that direct victimization by the counterinsurgency will be associated with *less* support for the insurgents. This contradicts the "hearts and minds" school of counterinsurgency. However, it is consistent with civilian incentives to adhere to authorities based on their territorial, clan-based embeddedness and high dependence on communal ties. These civilians are not fond of government authorities, to be certain, but they regard the insurgents as a much greater threat to themselves and their families. Therefore, civilians who report exposure to

---

[43] "Killings of Islamic Figures in the North Caucasus (2009–2016)," December 16, 2016, *Kavkazsky Uzel*, www.kavkaz-uzel.eu/articles/244966/.

[44] "On the Prohibition of Wahhabi and Other Extremist Activities in the Territory of the Republic of Dagestan." Law of Republic of Dagestan #15, September 22, 1999, http://docs.cntd.ru/docu ment/802037545.

direct counterinsurgent violence will be forced into compliance and indicate less support for the insurgency. This leads to the second proposition that, all else equal:

(H1b) direct governmental violence *decreases* support for the insurgency

Some unfortunate individuals will be directly victimized by both the insurgency and the counterinsurgency. In Dagestan, one such category of individuals that is likely to have been targeted by both sides covers Muslims who visit the so-called "Salafi mosques." The counterinsurgency in Dagestan frequently detains, "registers," and harasses such worshipers.[45] At the same time, some of these individuals might also experience unfriendly (i.e., violent) encounters with rival insurgent factions, especially at this time in the conflict when infighting in the Dagestani "rebelocracy" was commonplace (Arjona 2016). Given the fact that their religious affinity, and their adherence to Salafism (as opposed to secular or Sufi counterinsurgents), puts these victims more in the rebel "segment," we expect that respondents exposed to *both* direct insurgent and counterinsurgent violence will indicate greater support for insurgency. This leads to the third version of the first hypothesis that, all else equal:

(H1c) exposure to direct insurgent *and* counterinsurgent violence *increases* support for the insurgency

In addition to these three core hypotheses about the effects of direct violence on civilian support for the insurgency, we assess a second set of hypotheses about the effects of ***indirect*** violence. By indirect violence or indirect victimization, we mean that the respondent did not experience the violence directly, but heard about it through rumor, media, or hearsay. Direct and indirect victimization are qualitatively distinct, we submit, and therefore generate differential effects on civilian attitudes toward insurgency. Whereas direct victimization entails a lived experience with a concrete (harmful) interaction with either the rebels or the counterinsurgents, indirect victimization is based on perception and hearsay, and therefore subject to both information network bias and cognitive dissonance. When faced with indirect violence, civilians tend to seek out and interpret information in a way that confirms one's prior beliefs – a well-known psychological phenomenon known as "confirmation bias" (Knobloch-Westerwick, Johnson, and Westerwick 2015; Nickerson 1998).

---

[45] Ilyas Kapiev, "Visitors to the Mosque in Makhachkala Voiced Problems Related to Profiling." *Kavkazsky Uzel*, March 6, 2020, www.kavkaz-uzel.eu/articles/346781/.

Since victimization is usually perceived as negative, we conjecture that civilians will assign the blame for it according to their sympathies. In other words, actors who are perceived negatively will be blamed for committing violence and those who are perceived positively will not be deemed liable. We therefore expect civilians who report hearing that rebels victimized villagers elsewhere (indirect violence) to reduce their support for the insurgency. Recall that this represents the opposite to direct violence, which we postulated would result in greater support for the perpetrator. We predict that civilians exposed to hearsay about counterinsurgent violence (indirect exposure) should express greater support for the insurgency, and vice versa, those who report hearing about insurgent violence will express less support for the rebels.

In sum, we expect indirect counterinsurgent violence to push civilians further into the arms of the insurgency, where their sympathies lie anyway, while indirect insurgent violence should push civilians, who are most likely already predisposed to dislike the rebels, even further away from them. This expectation is also consistent with "construal level theory" in social psychology, which predicts that people use a more abstract level of perception when evaluating temporally, spatially, and socially distant events (Liberman, Trope, and Stephan 2007; Trope and Liberman 2003).

In other contexts (e.g., Afghanistan; see Lyall et al. 2013), researchers have found that the effect of exposure to violence on individual-level support for the insurgency "fades away" as the "distance" from violence diminishes – that is, from direct exposure to indirect experiences. This implies that the size of the action's effect ought to decrease as respondents move from direct exposure to violence to indirect experiences based on hearsay. To put it differently, indirect violence is simply a lesser form of direct violence, and the intensity of the support is inversely proportionate to the "distance" from violence.

We posit instead that exposure to indirect violence is qualitatively different than exposure to direct violence. Direct victimization entails a personal experience that is imbued with information received directly through the interaction with either the rebels or with the counterinsurgents. By contrast, indirect victimization is based on a pre-existing opinion that is applied to understand a rumor. The more distant the event, the more abstraction and event construction is involved to make sense of it (Liberman, Trope, and Stephan 2007; Trope and Liberman 2003), which implies that the person is more likely to rely on his/her preexisting beliefs. The resulting judgment about each side is thus subject to both information network bias (e.g., Kosta 2019) and cognitive dissonance. In a situation where someone "hears about violence," civilians tend to seek out and interpret information in a way that confirms their prior beliefs from their respective viewpoints about the actors involved, which implies that civilians believe the "other side" is responsible for any indirect violence about which they have heard rumors. As a result, they attribute blame to the other "silo" and reduce their support accordingly.

This understanding of the distinction between these forms of exposure to violence implies that a shift from direct to indirect violence involves a difference in the *direction* of the effect, not just a change in the magnitude. But both groups, it is important to emphasize, are already in these camps, which is why they attribute the indirect violence to the other actor in the first place. For these reasons, indirect violence is predicted to increase support for the insurgency if the government is "responsible" for it, but to decrease support for the insurgency if the insurgency is "culpable."

Finally, we expect that those civilians who report indirect violence by both sides will mostly stick to the rebel side. With indirect victimization, we identify two main types of distance between observers (civilians) and events (violence): spatial and cultural (Linke and O'Loughlin 2015).[46] There is a spatial distance between the observer and the event, since these civilians are not directly affected by violence, and there is cultural distance between the civilians and the perpetrators. On average, since the counterinsurgency forces will tend to be viewed as slightly more culturally distant vis-à-vis civilians, respondents are more likely to rely on their pre-existing biases and knowledge when assessing indirect counterinsurgent violence (Knobloch-Westerwick, Johnson, and Westerwick 2015; Liberman, Trope, and Stephan 2007; Nickerson 1998; Trope and Liberman 2003). This reasoning implies the additional following three interrelated hypotheses regarding the effects of indirect violence:

(H2a) indirect insurgent violence *decreases* support for the insurgency

(H2b) indirect counterinsurgency violence *increases* support for the insurgency

(H2c) exposure to indirect violence from *both* the insurgency and counterinsurgency *increases* support for the insurgency

Table 1 summarizes these hypotheses.

3.2 Alternative Explanations

In addition to examining the effect of exposure to violence, which forms the theoretical focus of this study, we also consider several other important factors highlighted in the scholarly literature.

---

[46] For more on distance and context, see this important article, which reconceptualizes and theorizes distance, and then uses survey data from the North Caucasus to assess it.

Table 1 The hypothesized relationships between type and source of
victimization and support for the insurgency

	Type of victimization	
	Direct victimization	**Indirect victimization**
Source of victimization	**Support for Insurgency**	
Insurgency	High	Low
Counterinsurgency	Low	High
Both	High	High

The first factor is poverty, which numerous studies of insurgency, rebel groups, and civil war have emphasized. According to one school of reasoning, poverty is thought to create the conditions for recruitment to insurgent groups due to lower opportunity costs (Besley and Persson 2011; Miguel, Satyanath, and Sergenti 2004) and greater susceptibility and grievances (Sambanis 2005; Van Acker 2004). However, using micro-level research designs and data, other scholars have found that poorer people have less favorable attitudes toward insurgent groups than members of the middle class (Blair, Fair, Malhotra, and Shapiro 2013; Fair and Shepherd 2006), calling into question our understanding of this important relationship. Some researchers have even found that wealthier individuals and those with pro-democracy attitudes are more likely to support insurgents (Shapiro and Fair 2009). While poorer countries are also widely thought to have higher levels of political violence (Miguel, Satyanath, and Sergenti 2004), recent analysis indicates that the evidence remains less disposi-tive at the micro-level (Blattman and Miguel 2010).[47]

The middle class and wealthier families also appear heavily overrepresented in terms of direct participation as the perpetrators of violence, suggesting that economic grievance due to poverty may not be a primary motivation, at least for participation (Krueger and Malečková 2003), which is of course distinct from support. Some studies have suggested that the middle class might have the right combination of grievances and opportunities to push for political change and seek different rule (Siroky, Dzutsev, and Hechter 2013). To account for these potentially ambiguous effects, we have included an indicator of self-reported income to assess whether support for rebels is correlated with economic status. In addition, we account for retrospective economic evaluations.

---

[47] This distinction between macro- and micro-level findings is one that has affected much of the literature but its implications have yet to be adequately explored and addressed.

Second, many studies recognize ethnic identity as a factor that shapes civilian attitudes toward the insurgency. Ethnicity can serve to reduce uncertainty regarding future actions (Hale 2008) and can provide a strong sense of ethnic responsibility (Aliyev 2019). Mironova and Whitt (2018), in a study of Kosovo, show that civilians sharing an ethnic identity with the government or with the insurgency are much more likely to support them.[48] Ethnic identity plays a significant role in Dagestan, as previous studies have demonstrated (Kisriev and Ware 2006; Holland and O'Loughlin 2010). It is crucial therefore to include an indicator of whether the respondents belong to one of the two largest ethnic groups during this time period (Dargins or Avars), which respectively ruled Dagestan before and during the survey. We also examine how belonging to one of these ethnic groups may *interact* with exposure to violence to shape civilian support for the insurgency.[49]

At the micro-level, we emphasize how being a member of one of the two ethnic groups – Avar or Dargin, which together constitute about 50 percent of the population – shaped civilian support for the insurgency.[50] We have data on other groups as well, but we theorize that membership in these groups should have distinct effects, since Dargins (Magomedsalam Magomedov, a Dargin leader of the republic) lost power in January 2013 to an Avar (Ramazan Abdulatipov) due to the political reshuffle by the Kremlin. We expect that there is greater support for insurgents among Dargins than Avars, all else equal (since the former lost power to the latter), and greater support among Avars or Dargins than among members of other groups such as Kumyks, Lezghins, etc.

Third, since the insurgency movement in Dagestan was undoubtedly based on Islamic slogans, and religiosity is one of the crucial factors dividing the civilian population in Dagestan, we include an ordinal indicator of the religiosity of respondents – specifically, the frequency of *namaz* or *salah* (prayers performed by Muslims): from "no prayer" at all to "five times per day." We considered asking about belonging to a Salafi order, but our discussions with the local research team suggested that the security hazards faced by Salafists in Russia and especially in Dagestan rendered such a question too dangerous for the respondents to answer truthfully or even for enumerators to ask directly, and

---

[48] Power asymmetry, which characterizes most wars of insurgency but especially so in Dagestan, can enhance this effect, which operates as an adaptive survival mechanism for individuals to manage risk in irregular wars when their own group is under threat (Hewstone, Rubin, and Willis 2002).

[49] We interact ethnicity of the respondent and the type of exposure to violence they experienced: cf. Figure 10 and Figure 11 in the empirical analysis chapter.

[50] Russian Census in Dagestan (2010): Avars 29% Dargin 17%, Kumyk 15%, Lezgin 13%, Laks 6%, other groups are less than 5%.

therefore we determined that asking about *namaz* was the most acceptable alternative.

Finally, we also considered other factors that have received attention in the relevant literatures, including political and religiously based grievances. To examine the potential political grievances of respondents, we asked civilians whether they think the central authorities of Russia are doing a good job of helping solve Dagestan's problems; we also asked whether respondents think that the Russian authorities are doing a good job of protecting the rights of Muslims.[51] Finally, we included measures of respondent-level education (level), age (in years), gender (male/female), and settlement type (urban/ rural). We expect that younger and more rural individuals will be more likely to support the insurgency than older and more urban individuals. We do not expect gender to have a consistent and clear effect. The inclusion of these alternative explanations does not change the main findings, and in some cases provided important insights.

After describing our theory and the hypotheses that we seek to test, it should be apparent that using direct questions and regular surveys was not feasible, or was at least highly risky. We therefore began to consider the alternative approaches that are available to researchers for probing sensitive topics and doing experiments in dangerous research settings using more unobtrusive questioning techniques. The next section discusses these approaches, and explains why we ultimately selected one of them to pursue.

4 Which Experiment to Choose?

This Element builds on qualitative and quantitative research about the insurgency in the Caucasus (e.g., Bakke, O'Loughlin, Toal, and Ward 2014; Dzutsati, Siroky, and Dzutsev 2016; Linke and O'Loughlin 2015; O'Loughlin, Holland, and Witmer 2011; Ratelle and Souleimanov 2017; Siroky, Dzutsev, and Hechter 2013; Souleimanov and Aliyev 2015; Toft and Zhukov 2012; Ware and Kisriev 2009; Zhukov 2012). These studies served as crucial material in the decision to utilize indirect questioning techniques in order to partly overcome the challenge of obtaining reliable answers about supporting the insurgents, determining which technique was most appropriate for this problem and research setting, adapting and designing it (including the choice of neutral but realistic terminology and the choice of "controls," or, in our case, "policies"), and developing

---

[51] These last three variables did not improve out-of-sample prediction using information criteria, and are excluded from the main model in the Element, but presented in the Appendix.

the overall survey to cover not only our theoretical focus but also relevant factors highlighted in prior studies.[52]

In order to safeguard the identities of all respondents and diminish the chances of retribution, researchers and enumerators can do several things. In our view, the most important are: conducting interviews in private settings; separating names from other identifying information, such as age, gender, village, etc.; and matching enumerators to respondents on other demographic characteristics. One extra step to protect all those involved is to avoid collecting geographic information on the respondents, especially if data are being collected in small, tight-knit, easy-to-identify communities such as villages.[53]

Regional knowledge and qualitative research helped us on the front end to determine the feasibility of the study, and on the back end to interpret the results in a manner consistent with what we know from regional and subject matter expertise. Combining qualitative evidence with experiments and other kinds of multi-method research has become an increasingly sophisticated norm in the social sciences. Guidance on how to do so most effectively is increasingly being discussed in the literature on multi-method research (Dunning 2012; Levy Paluck 2010; Lieberman 2005; Seawright 2016; 2020; Weller and Barnes 2014). Qualitative research can significantly contribute, *inter alia*, to our ability to interpret the treatment by providing "the narrative material to convey the results to broader audiences, the reasons for differences in causal effects, and the measurement of key elements in the design, and works best when it is used interactively on equal footing with other methods, and when 'each method is used for its strengths'" (Seawright 2021, 384).

That it would even be possible for us to implement a survey in Dagestan was not at all a given. Access to civilians in Dagestan – like in many other counterinsurgency campaigns in strong authoritarian regimes – is severely restricted, and researchers must take this into account as a practical matter, a research design consideration, and a safety issue. The Russian government's aggressive, and often abusive, counterinsurgency campaign in this peripheral,

---

[52] On "psychological realism," see Aronson, Wilson, and Brewer (1998, p. 132).

[53] This is the conservative approach that we selected because we wanted to be certain that the data could never be matched back to the individuals or their villages in the event of a data breach, and we wanted respondents to know this so they would feel more trust toward the enumerators and the project. While this naturally hindered our ability to make comparisons with actual violence in different localities, by using matched observational data, and prevented us from conducting other kinds of spatial analysis, we felt that at this time it was crucial to ensuring the safety of all respondents. Such tradeoffs in favor of security over the advantages from collecting more detailed data are not uncommon in this kind of research, where the first principle of the research must be some form of the Hippocratic Oath: first, do no harm. Other studies have in fact linked spatial data to individual data (Linke and O'Loughlin 2015), but their survey was done in 2005, which was a different context than ten years later.

Muslim-majority region meant that eliciting truthful answers represented a challenge regardless of the method we selected – no methodology can ever truly overcome the limits and constraints imposed by a conspicuously desperate situation. In some North Caucasian regions, such as Chechnya that lies just west of Dagestan, implementing a survey of this kind even with indirect questioning would be impracticable (Souleimanov et al. 2019). However, although Dagestan is extremely violent and dangerous by most research standards, it was still feasible to conduct research at the time of our study in 2015.

Government-imposed penalties even for expressing verbal support toward the insurgency made our decision to rule out a direct question on support for the insurgency and to consider only indirect techniques that much simpler. While direct questioning techniques may indeed suffice in other settings, especially if the topic is not overly delicate or too problematic to speak about publicly, this was not (and still is not) the case in Dagestan. Direct questioning represented too great a risk in terms of safety, and was likely to produce excessive non-response and various forms of sensitivity bias. We therefore considered other options, which we discuss in the following sections, beginning with endorsement experiments that we ultimately decided to use for this study.

4.1 Endorsement Experiments

After carefully considering the available techniques for soliciting information from Dagestani civilians about support for sensitive political actors, we opted for *endorsement experiments* over other possible indirect questioning techniques, such as randomized response technique, unmatched count or list experiments, and the sealed envelope method (Gingerich 2010; Imai 2011; Lyall et al. 2013; Raghavarao and Federer 1979; Tsuchiya et al. 2007; Warner 1965). Our choice was driven by previous scholarship, by our knowledge of the region, and by discussions with our colleagues on the ground in Dagestan about the approach that was most likely to succeed. Using this domain knowledge, we then selected the policies for the experiments, the term to use for describing the insurgents, and other aspects of the design.[54]

---

[54] The costs entail designing and implementing the experiments; reduced sample size by a factor equal to the number of endorsement and control groups, typically two; and obtaining an indirect rather than a direct measure to interpret.

The primary advantages we sought by using this technique were: (1) greater safety for respondents and enumerators, (2) higher likelihood of eliciting a truthful response/lower likelihood of social desirability bias, and (3) increased response rates/lower non-response. A key advantage of the endorsement technique is that it never asks about support for the sensitive object or actor itself, and it does not require the respondent to name it or to count it. This puts the respondents at less risk and, in theory, should make them more likely to provide truthful responses, thereby substantially reducing non-response rates (Matanock and García-Sánchez 2018). In a rare validation study (Rosenfeld et al. 2016), the endorsement approach performed better or as good as the other methods on these criteria, especially the ability to reduce sensitivity bias, lower non-response, and protect respondents, while probing taboo topics.[55]

The set-up of the endorsement experiment is relatively simple, which is also part of its attraction, especially for low-information and low-cognitive-capacity environments. The survey is split into two parts, usually with an equal number of respondents. In the experimental version, respondents are told that the sensitive political actor "endorses" a policy. Later, we discuss how we selected the policies, but for now we just provide an example. One of the items in our survey was support for polygamy (a policy), and in the experimental version it was "endorsed" by insurgents (the sensitive actor), whereas there is no mention of the sensitive political actor in the control version, just the policy. The respondent's "support," even in the treatment version, could thus indicate either support for the controversial policy or for the sensitive actor, and in this way it is protected from the adverse consequences of expressing support directly. Taking the difference in the average policy preferences across the two groups (experimental and control) provides a latent measure of support for the political actor.[56]

A seminal example of this approach was implemented in Lyall et al. (2013), which studied support for the ISAF counterinsurgency and the Taliban in Afghanistan, and has been applied also in Pakistan. In conflict settings such as these, endorsement experiments have proven particularly useful for probing support for sensitive political actors, but there were also three other techniques that we considered but ultimately rejected for this particular study, for reasons we describe in the following sections.

---

[55] For RRT versus direct questioning, see a meta-meta-analysis that covered two other meta-analyses of thirty-two comparative studies and six validations: Lensvelt-Mulders, Hox, van der Heijden, and Maas 2005.

[56] Other indirect questioning techniques exploit aggregation or noise to veil respondents' sensitive attitudes and behaviors, but often directly call to mind the sensitive item, attitude, or behavior.

4.2 Randomized Response Technique

We considered three other indirect questioning techniques that have been widely used in the social sciences. The first is the randomized response technique (RRT), which protects respondents by making it impossible to precisely identify individual responses through the addition of a randomizing device such as a die, coin, or random number generator (Horvitz, Shah, and Simmons 1967; Lamb and Stem 1978; Locander, Sudman, and Bradburn 1976; Warner 1965; Tracy and Fox 1981; Rosenfeld et al. 2016; cf. Takhasi and Sakasegawa 1977 for a version without a randomizing device). Only when the randomization device produces certain outcomes does the respondent answer truthfully (for example, the coin shows tails). If not (for example, if the coin is heads), the respondent answers as instructed beforehand by the enumerator. The researchers explore the gap in answers between the population that answered as instructed and the population that answered truthfully. The enumerator does not see the outcome, and thus does not know if the respondent is answering truthfully or not. This method works by introducing uncertainty through *noise*, which is driven by the randomization device utilized.

This is a good approach when the population being surveyed is highly educated and the risk of responding positively to the question is not life-threatening. We determined that this technique was less likely to be effective in our context for four reasons. First, it assumes a level of education and compliance with the randomization procedure that seemed to us unrealistically demanding in Dagestan, especially in villages. Second, and more importantly, it requires the respondent to directly say "yes" to indicate support, and doing so in Dagestan carried considerable risks that we deemed unacceptable. Third, randomization devices are reminiscent of gambling, which is a culturally sensitive issue in Dagestan. Fourth, previous work also indicated that the randomized response method can generate a higher non-response rate than other indirect methods (Lensvelt-Mulders et al. 2005), and we were very concerned about high non-response rates as well as attrition.

4.3 Unmatched Count Technique

The second alternative approach that we considered using was the unmatched count technique (UCT), which is also known as the list experiment or the item-count technique because it asks respondents to count the number of "yes" answers on a list.[57] One version lists the sensitive actor and the other does

---

[57] For a meta-analysis of list experiments in political science, see Blair, Coppock, and Moor (2020).

not, so the difference in the average number of "yes" answers between the two groups is an indirect measure of support for the sensitive actor. It hides individual responses and introduces uncertainty through *aggregation*. This technique is useful when the level of risk to the respondents for saying "all" or "none" is within an acceptable range. However, there are some disadvantages, which caused us to favor endorsement experiments instead, and could cause others considering their use in warzones to reevaluate their choice. A key problem is that those respondents who count either "zero" or "all" of the options are not at all protected, since their count indicates either "no support" or "support" for the sensitive actor or item.

Consistent with this intuition, it is noteworthy that not a single respondent to the item count experiments done in the study of civilian support for militants and foreign forces in Afghanistan (out of almost 3,000) answered "zero" or "all" (Blair 2020, p. 15). This strongly indicates that respondents may see through the flaws of this technique and protect themselves by not answering truthfully. While Blair and Imai (2012), as well as others, have developed methods to identify and address this problem, it still does not fully solve the issue of social desirability bias (Blair, Coppock, and Moor 2020), which seems to be worse for list experiments than for either the randomized response or endorsement approaches. Compared to endorsement experiments, we also felt that both the randomized response and item count techniques were less intuitive procedures for a context such as Dagestan.[58]

4.4 Sealed Envelope Method

Finally, there is also the sealed envelope method (SEM), sometimes called the "Secret Ballot Approach" (SBA). This can be conducted in different ways, but one of the most common methods involves face-to-face implementation, with a sealed envelope being given to the respondents at the end of the session. No randomization is required, but this approach is often combined with another method of asking the question and then compared to SEM in order to assess the prevalence of the sensitive item or behavior in the population (Gregson et al. 2002; Juarez et al. 2010). The envelope can contain any number of sensitive items. The responses can also vary, from a simple circling of "yes" or "no" to a more complicated scale. For less literate audiences, pictures can be used instead of words. The respondent is told to fold their paper and put it in the envelope after they have finished. In the meantime, the interviewers backs are

---

[58] For application of the item count or list in political science, see the meta-analysis by Blair et al. (2020); and for design issues in lists, see Corstange (2009), Glynn (2013), and Aronow et al. (2013).

turned to the respondents (unless this is culturally inappropriate) or they go into another room so that the respondents actions are not observed. The intention is to reduce the incentives to conceal by introducing uncertainty through *anonymity*.

This approach has the advantage of being very low-tech and having low cognitive requirements. In addition, compared to the randomized response technique, it has the benefit that data from the sensitive questions can be linked back to other information about the respondents, and that it can be self-administered. However, the SEM is also subject to potential abuse: for example, if the interviewee does not put the sealed envelope into a box or bag with many others, thereby ensuring the preservation of anonymity. If, for example, the sealed envelope is taken alone, it can be later marked and deanonymized.

Having briefly described four different approaches to probing sensitive topics, along with some variations of them, we next summarize and briefly review their main advantages and disadvantages.

4.5 Advantages and Disadvantages

Table 2 systematically compares the general features, and also notes the particular advantages and disadvantages, of direct and four indirect questioning techniques.[59] The place to begin is with the problem(s) these methods are designed to address. The two primary problems for which these methods were largely designed are non-response bias and inaccurate response or sensitivity bias (also known as not answering truthfully). All of them are therefore potentially useful for studying sensitive issues in dangerous settings, but each has unique advantages and disadvantages. Validation studies are rare, and sometimes not possible precisely where they would be needed, but we can learn from those that have been conducted recently.[60]

On the first big issue of non-response bias, validation studies indicate that the endorsement experiment approach is among the best options – if not the very best (see Table 2). List experiments are a close second on this count, and randomized response a distant third. Direct questions on sensitive topics, not surprisingly, are by far the weakest in this regard. The sealed envelope method was not considered in the validations, so it is difficult to rank it in the same way, but it stands to reason that (at least the non-self-administered version) would do well with non-response, certainly much better than a direct question and potentially just as well as the top performers (endorsements and lists).

---

[59] Isaqzadeh, Gulzar, and Shapiro (2020) and Graeme (2018) also provide useful tables that summarize and compare these methods.

[60] Ranking of bias reduction (recovers true estimates) and non-response reduction is based on a validation study by Rosenfeld et al. (2016).

Table 2 Comparison of experimental approaches for surveying sensitive subjects

Method	Sensitivity Bias Reduction (Truthful Responses)	Non-response Reduction	Protection of Respondents	Cognitive Requirements	Main Drawbacks	Main Advantages	Indirect Technique
Direct Question	(5) Worst	(5) Worst	(5) Worst	Low	High non-response rate and sensitivity bias	Easy to understand, implement, low cost, no loss of statistical power	None
Item Count or List Experiment	(4)	(2)	(4)	Medium	- Floor and Ceiling Effects - Does not obscure all responses or protect respondents for "all" or "none" answers	Does not require naming sensitive object, actor, or item	Introduces uncertainty through aggregation
Randomized Response Method – RRM (disguised and forced)	(1) Best	(4) Much worse than Item Count	(2)	High	- Requires respondent participation for randomization, which leads to higher non-response and attrition - Slightly harder to explain - Games of chance may be culturally inappropriate	Useful for estimating population-level variables. Good protection of responses	Introduces uncertainty through noise

Table 2 (cont.)

Method	Sensitivity Bias Reduction (Truthful Responses)	Non-response Reduction	Protection of Respondents	Cognitive Requirements	Main Drawbacks	Main Advantages	Indirect Technique
Sealed Envelope Method	(3)	(3)	(3)	Low	- Prone to abuse - Still underestimates sensitive trait	- Low cognitive requirements - Low cost to add - Computational ease	Introduces uncertainty through anonymity
Endorsement Experiment	(2) Close to RRM	(1) Best	(1) Best	Low	- Inefficient estimation and latent variable model. - No obvious scale (like Likert)	- High level of plausible deniability for respondents - Reduced vulnerability for enumerators	Obscures the object of evaluation and researcher intention

When it comes to reducing sensitivity bias (or, conversely, eliciting truthful responses), the endorsement experiments and randomized response approaches came a close second and first, respectively. The list experiment was third, but was still better than the direct question. The sealed envelope option was not considered in this validation study, but it ought to perform well on reducing sensitivity bias, provided that protocols protect anonymity – that is, the respondents see their envelope mixed with other similar unlabeled envelopes, and so are assured that their ballot will remain anonymous.

The educational and cultural context in which the study occurs plays an important role in selecting which method to use. The randomized response, for example, requires the use of dice, coins, or some other randomization technique, and in some settings games of chance are deemed culturally inappropriate. It also has the highest cognitive-ability requirements which, when not met, can result in high non-response and attrition rates.[61] The item count requires significantly less education to be effective (basic counting), while the endorsement experiment and the sealed envelope method do not have any demanding cognitive requirements to work properly and have been deployed successfully in low-information environments.

The sensitivity and nature of the topic being investigated can also play a role in selecting the most appropriate method. Whereas the randomized response technique is not generally thought to be effective for highly sensitive topics as it only introduces some uncertainty through noise, which the enumerators and researchers can then extract if they know the distribution of the randomization procedure.[62] The list version is somewhat better in this regard, as it does not require the respondent to name the sensitive thing, just to count it along with other items, but floor and ceiling effects make list experiments challenging.[63] The sealed envelope method has been used for highly sensitive topics (e.g., AIDS prevalence, sexual promiscuity, etc.), and has been shown to work well in these environments (Juarez et al. 2010).

Endorsement experiments appear to offer one of the most promising approaches for studying taboo subjects that may be illegal to disclose or that

---

[61] On design and analysis to increase compliance, see Gingerich (2010) and Blair, Imai and Zhou (2015).

[62] The disguised version of the RRM might be slightly preferable to the forced version in this regard, but both approaches are poorly suited to highly intrusive topics that could get respondents killed, such as support for the insurgency.

[63] Glynn (2013) discusses the problem of ceiling effects, and reduced noise, in list experiments, and offers some possible remedies; see also Blair and Imai (2012). Nonetheless, some studies have used this method successfully and found no floor or ceiling effects. Frye et al. 2017, for example, use lists to estimate the actual popular support for President Putin, and found no floor effects. They conclude that Putin's support is indeed "real" and hovers around 80 percent. For a review, see Blair, Coppock and Moor (2020).

could get respondents killed.[64] The endorsement experiment has a major advantage in that it not only obscures the object of evaluation but also hides the researcher's intention, and it does not require naming or counting anything. It gives the respondent the most plausible deniability, provided the policies are well designed for the context, which means greater safety for respondents. At the same time that it protects respondents, it also minimizes the vulnerability of enumerators. These are key considerations when conducting studies of sensitive topics in dangerous settings.

It is important to recognize that indirect questioning is not a panacea: it has its limitations and poses its own issues. All these methods try to reduce the cost and risk of answering truthfully, but none of them can compel people to answer if they do not wish to do so, and none imposes any cost for not responding sincerely. One important drawback of such techniques is the loss of efficiency in estimation compared to direct questions. There are technical fixes to reduce the efficiency-loss problem, and a larger sample size is often needed to gain adequate statistical power.[65]

To increase power in endorsement experiments, for example, one can ask multiple policy questions and combine them for analysis (see Lyall, Blair, and Imai 2013), as we do in the next section. This requires identifying policies that all relate to the same latent dimension and on which the sensitive actors can be reasonably linked, but at the same time must not be exclusively associated with the sensitive actors in a way that would tip off the respondents and render the manipulation worthless. Other solutions, specifically for increasing power with list experiments, include the "double list experiment" for item count techniques (Glynn 2013), combining direct questions and lists (Aronow et al. 2013), and asking the control items individually for the control group (Corstange 2009). List experiments can also be combined with endorsement experiments. While some studies suggest that the two methods unveil very similar patterns of political behavior among civilians (see Blair, Imai, and Lyall 2014), others have found that endorsement experiments and randomized response techniques

---

[64] Provided that the policies are well designed such that they cannot be exclusively associated with the sensitive actor(s), but are plausibly linked to the actor(s).

[65] When the population joint distribution of covariates is available, post-stratification can be used for estimating levels of support for groups in question in the population to improve the efficiency of the estimation (Park, Gelman, and Bafumi 2017; Bullock, Imai, and Shapiro 2011). However, in Dagestan, as in many conflict-ridden and authoritarian contexts, census data are either publicly unavailable or misrepresented. Specifically, in Dagestan, the authorities appear to exaggerate the overall population of the territory and to manipulate shares of ethnic groups. The first is done to receive more funding from the central government; the second to safeguard positions of power of certain ethnic groups and their representatives. See, for example, Marko Shakhbanov, "Russians, Azeris, Highlanders: Why are the Results of the Dagestan Census Distorted?" *Regnum*, February 10, 2012, https://regnum.ru/news/polit/1497900.html.

produce the least bias, as compared to list experiments and direct questions (Rosenfeld et al. 2016).

One can also validate experimental studies by matching and comparing results to census data, social media data, and other forms of observational data. Several studies have effectively done this already (e.g., Rosenfeld et al. 2016). When it comes to conflict research, such validation using census data is often difficult to conduct. As a result, most research on civil wars has focused on the armed rebels and their observable actions, including against civilians, which rarely (if ever) involves probing the attitudes of any of the actors involved (armed or unarmed), and instead draws on observational group-region-country level data rather than on systematic micro-level data.

Finally, another issue that arises is the loss in interpretability, which is arguably the case for endorsement experiments specifically as a result of the latent variable model and the lack of a natural scale. At the same time, most interpretation of data depends on behavioral assumptions that are not always testable. In addition to extensive pre-testing, when feasible, another solution to the problem of interpretation lies in bringing in area expertise and domain knowledge, which can provide a baseline against which to evaluate responses and exclude improbable interpretations. Such expertise and knowledge, which is often based on years of fieldwork, can help not only with interpretation but also with the design and identification of appropriate questions and wordings. In Dagestan in 2015, for example, we know that no areas of the republic were under the formal control of rebels. Therefore, we were certain that we could not interpret support for policies as mere compliance due to coercion. From area studies and other qualitative reports on the irregular war in Dagestan, we can validate this interpretation by verifying the considerable ideological alignment of civilians with the conflicting sides.

Knowing the situation on the ground and in historical context is probably the strongest logic of all for determining which method is most appropriate for a particular research question and location. The security situation in Dagestan took direct questioning off the table. Moreover, we determined that the RRT method was unlikely to work in a context with many rural areas and low education, due to compliance and attrition issues. Further, gambling is deemed culturally inappropriate to many in Dagestan, although people do practice it, and so randomization devices such as dice, cards, and coins would send the wrong message to the respondents and could lead to an additional increase in non-response.

The list approach, we reckoned, was also less likely to be effective due to similar studies in conflicts zones (e.g., Lyall et al. 2013) that found considerable floor and ceiling effects. Finally, the sealed envelope approach might have worked in this context, but based on conversations with our local colleagues, we were concerned that someone outside the sample might obtain (a copy of) one and somehow jeopardize the whole enterprise. By contrast, endorsement experiments, provided the policies are properly designed and the endorser label is sufficiently neutral, seemed most likely to reduce non-response bias and sensitivity bias, while not imposing high cognitive or other demands on the respondents and remaining culturally appropriate.

To summarize, this study investigates the correlates of civilian wartime attitudes toward the insurgency using micro-level data (individuals) and deploying an experimental design. Specifically, it estimates the latent level of civilian support for the insurgency, and the effect of civilian exposure due to direct and indirect violence at the hands of both the insurgency and the counterinsurgency.[66] While the collection of new individual-level data on such a highly sensitive topic could put the lives of those involved in danger, unobtrusive experimental techniques enable one to minimize this risk while obtaining accurate, if indirect, answers.

This strategy, if carefully conceived and implemented, can be successful in a diversity of contexts and on many topics that interest social scientists but have evaded systematic analysis due to the difficulty of obtaining reliable data. Which technique is most appropriate will ultimately depend on the specific context, but can and should be informed by the differences, advantages, and disadvantages of each of the approaches. Moreover, in some settings and circumstances, it may be prudent to combine the techniques, and methods to do so are now widely available.

The next section describes the survey experiment we ultimately designed for this setting and then discusses the core results. Specifically, it elaborates on the endorsement experiments, along with key covariates, and draws out lessons learned that we think may apply more generally.

5 The Endorsement Experiment

This section introduces our study of civilian support for the insurgency in Dagestan.[67] We discuss the endorsement experiment that we deployed for this study, the motivation for utilizing the endorsement experiment over other indirect questioning techniques, and the design of the policies for the experiment.

---

[66] For quite some time, survey experimental designs did not allow multivariate analysis. With the advent of new computational tools and greater focus on the use of such methods, researchers proposed ways to go beyond the examining of bivariate relationships. Now, methods and opensource software are available that significantly expand our ability to use experimental data (Corstange 2009; Blair and Imai 2012; Bullock, Imai, and Shapiro 2011).

[67] The design used here builds on seminal studies in the field (e.g., Blair and Imai 2012; Blair, Fair, Malhotra, and Shapiro 2013; Bullock, Imai, and Shapiro 2011; Chaudhuri and Christofides 2013; Lyall, Blair, and Imai 2013; Shiraito and Imai 2017).

After considering all of the available approaches to study this topic and similarly sensitive subjects, as discussed in the previous section, we opted for endorsement experiments. Our choice was driven, perhaps first and foremost, by discussions with colleagues on the ground in Dagestan about the approach that we believed most likely to succeed in this context. We found that discussing this important decision ex-ante with local researchers can narrow the range of options to the most optimal for a particular setting and research question. By success, we mean reducing non-response and sensitivity bias. As Section 4 indicates, existing validation studies and meta-analyses speak highly in favor of endorsement experiments as an approach to address these two important issues when dealing with highly sensitive subjects. Our choice was also driven in part by previous scholarship, which has successfully studied support for militant actors using endorsement experiments in other parts of the world. Fortunately, in this case, both sources of information pointed in the same direction.

Having settled on endorsement experiments, we then used context-specific knowledge and insights from discussions with our colleagues in the field to select and phrase five policy areas.[68] All five policy issues were selected because they could be *credibly but not exclusively* linked to the endorser – in this case, to the insurgency. This is not always easy, and often requires considering several options before settling on an optimal compromise. For example, it is possible to support energy independence (Policy 1 in the Appendix) without supporting the rebels, and vice versa (for example, the then governor of Dagestan, Ramazan Abdulatipov, advocated for the republic's ownership of local extractive industries),[69] but it is plausible that the rebels would promote energy independence as a means of reducing reliance on Moscow because they have separatist goals. In the treatment, the respondent is explicitly told that the policy is endorsed by the insurgents. However, since support for the policy itself is not necessarily another way of indicating support for the actor, the uncertainty introduced protects participants.

Another policy we selected was the acceptability of making profit on alcohol production. We knew from multiple sources that insurgents regularly attacked sellers of alcohol in Dagestan.[70] Clearly, the insurgency was strongly opposed to alcohol production and consumption. Opposition to alcohol consumption was not limited to militants, however, since Islam in general forbids drinking

---

[68] In the previous section, we note that one way to increase statistical power in endorsement experiments is to combine several policy issues.

[69] "Abdulatipov – RBK: 'There was no thief in the republic without a handler from Moscow,'" www.rbc.ru/politics/11/12/2018/5c0a5b499a7947c2ee25b704.

[70] "Dagestan: Chronicles of Terror 1996–2020," www.kavkaz-uzel.eu/articles/73122/; cf. Siroky et al. 2021.

alcohol along with using other intoxicants. At the same time, the republic hosted two renowned brandy factories in Kizlyar and Derbent, along with a few less-prominent alcohol-producing plants. Restaurants in the republic legally and openly served alcohol to their customers. These conditions in Dagestan provided us with the necessary conditions to exploit attitudes toward making money on alcohol production for one of the five policies.

Based on our local interlocutors' expertise and our research, we also had to decide on a name for the insurgency, with the goal of selecting a name that was relatively neutral in order not to introduce any bias via the terminology itself. We chose "[The] Forest Brothers" as a name for the insurgency as it had neither overly negative nor positive connotations in Dagestan.[71] However, it was clear to all whom the question was about – it was very comprehensive without being overly charged. In other words, terms for sensitive actors should balance neutrality with familiarity, and choose a name that is known but not patently partial. Based on these desiderata, we selected "[The] Forest Brothers." As a result, for our first policy question, we asked:

> Dagestan has significant energy resources, but they are not under republican control. *The "Forest Brothers"* think that if Dagestan were allowed to take control of its natural resources, it could help the republic develop economically. What do you think?

The control group was asked:

> Dagestan has significant energy resources, but they are not under republican control. **Some people think** that if Dagestan were allowed to take control of its natural resources, it could help the republic develop economically.

We picked policies that we believed were most likely to elicit truthful responses while affording respondents and enumerators maximal security. The decision of which policies to select is fraught with tension between the precision of measurement from the treatment to the outcome – support for the policy – and support for the endorser (Seawright 2021, p. 290). While seeking to balance policies that can be *credibly but not exclusively* linked to the sensitive actor, best practice uses domain knowledge and regional expertise to offer a mix of policies, some closer and some farther in the minds of respondents from being associated with the endorser. If the policy is too far from the endorser, it will either not be credible that the endorser actually endorses it, or it will attract too many respondents who support it but not the endorser, thereby rendering it harder to disentangle and uncover an accurate

---

[71] The term "Forest Brothers" apparently derives from the rebels in the Baltic states that fought against the Soviet government in 1944–1956 after the USSR occupied them.

impression of the latent level of support. If one chooses policies that are too closely associated with the endorser, then the experiment may not work well because supporters and sympathizers will understand the manipulation and be deterred from expressing support. The strategy of selecting a mix of "tight" and "loose" policies along one latent dimension provides more statistical power, which somewhat ameliorates the loss of power due to the experimental design. With all these considerations, it is clearly as much art as it is science.

The policies we selected were energy independence, ethnic quotas, monogamy, traditional healers, and an alcohol tax; we then aggregated them to generate an overall measure of latent support for the insurgency. Following standard procedure, the sample was divided into two groups using random assignment. The respondents in the control group were asked about support for the policies, measured using a 5-point Likert-scale, and treatment group respondents were asked identical questions, but with the "endorsement" of the policies from the "Forest Brothers." In the control case, the respondents are told just that "some people" support the policy in question (see Appendix).

The analysis then focuses on the difference in support for the five policies in the group with the specific endorsement (from the "Forest Brothers") and the group with a general endorsement from "some people". The logic of the endorsement experiment is based on the known bias in human judgment to evaluate things positively when placed beside or associated with something else that the individual thinks about positively. Of course, this also works in reverse with negative associations. Since assignment to the group endorsement is randomized, which is the crucial component, any difference in policy support is attributable exclusively to the group, because the specific endorsement is the sole distinction between the two versions of the question. This therefore offers an indicator of support for the insurgency.[72]

To understand and examine how support might be related to civilian exposure to wartime violence, both direct and indirect, we asked two questions. First, we asked respondents whether they or someone in their family had "suffered injury due to the actions of the militants" or "due to the actions of government forces" (we call this "direct exposure to violence").[73] In addition to assessing any potential asymmetry in the effect, due to the party responsible for the "direct"

---

[72] This approach is based on systematic research in social psychology on how the source of the information shapes the likelihood of persuasion (Cialdini 1984). As Blair et al. (2013, p. 37) put it: "the effectiveness of an endorsement in shifting views on a policy indicates the level of support for the endorser." We employ the same methodology as Bullock, Imai, and Shapiro (2011), which combines answers from the five endorsement experiments. The result is a latent measure of each respondent's support for the insurgency, which allows each question to have its own intercept but to share information about the effect of the predictors.

[73] Since familial, clan-based links in Dagestan tend to be quite expansive, and family members could include cousins, nieces, in-laws, and beyond, we designed the questions on direct victimization to allow for both personal victimization and victimization of a family member.

violence, we also examine whether the effect of exposure remains the same, attenuates (as previous studies found), or reverses (as we predict) when it is "indirect" exposure to violence. To understand exposure to indirect violence, we asked whether the respondents had "heard of anyone in the broader village/city suffering physical harm," due to the actions of the militants or due to the actions of government forces.

The survey organization and the interviewers took precautions to avoid "contamination" by exposing respondents to one another, which was all the more important in this context (with many small villages where people know one another well and are frequently related) because it could increase the security risk to respondents.[74]

5.1 Implementing an Endorsement Experiment

Russian Dagestan offers a difficult, but a rich arena for exploring the subtle relationships between civilians, rebels, and the government in an authoritarian setting. Using endorsement experiments and fine-grained data, we sought to assess how general theories elucidated the degree to which civilians support the insurgency, and the factors that shaped their support. The survey was completed in Dagestan in June 2015, by the Institute of Socio-Political Research, which is a part of the Russian Academy of Sciences. It relied upon multistage stratified probability sampling with two strata (territorial and quotidian).[75] The regionally representative household-based survey included 602 households. The enumerators were matched to respondents, both on ethnicity and on gender. Although the sample size is somewhat small given that endorsement experiments entail some efficiency loss, our use of five different endorsement experiments partly makes up for this, and provides adequate statistical power to detect effects at conventional alpha levels for a population size of less than 3 million (equivalent to Kansas).[76]

---

[74] We concede, however, that we could not fully rule out violations of the stable unit treatment value assumptions (SUTVA) (Rubin 1980), for respondents could have communicated among themselves, especially in smaller Dagestani villages, although the speed with which the survey was implemented in different villages somewhat mitigated this issue. Moreover, due to the sensitive nature of the subject and difficulties in gaining access to respondents, our ability to conduct in-depth interview with respondents was highly limited (Seawright 2021, p.391).

[75] Gender, age, education, and ethnicity.

[76] The survey covered twenty-six settlements (five towns, including the regional center, and twenty-one villages). Rural and urban areas were given an equal sampling weight, since they approximately reflect the population distribution in Dagestan. Makhachkala was oversampled, because a large part of insurgency activities took place in the city and its suburbs. The response rate was 35 percent. Most non-responses resulted from unattainable respondents, not refusals. Remote counties in the southwest and north were excluded from the sampling frame, along with several other villages, due to small population size and security considerations (e.g., Gimry, Novosasitli).

In each sampled household, data was collected via a face-to-face interview from one randomly selected individual, male or female, aged 18–86, who is a usual resident of that household (see Figure 4 and Figure 5 for demographic balance across the treatment and control samples). In addition to the conceptual modules related to exposure to violence, we also recorded economic, social, political, and demographic data on respondents. The formulation of specific questionnaire items built on prior work conducted in the North Caucuses, consultation with our local colleagues, and prior survey experiments about the determinants of civilian support for insurgencies in other parts of the world.

Since our main objective was to investigate the correlates of support for the insurgency with a focus on exposure to wartime violence, we focused on identifying individuals who had experienced direct and indirect exposure to violence. We also had the opportunity to inquire about a number of other factors that we intended to include as covariates in the statistical model. Religion was one of the hallmarks of the conflict in Dagestan. The arrival of Salafism (in the 1990s) was the primary ideational fissure that affected the creation and evolution of the insurgency in the republic. According to some researchers, the spread of new religious practices in Dagestan was brought about by the opening up of Russia to the world at the end of the 1980s. Thousands of Dagestanis went for

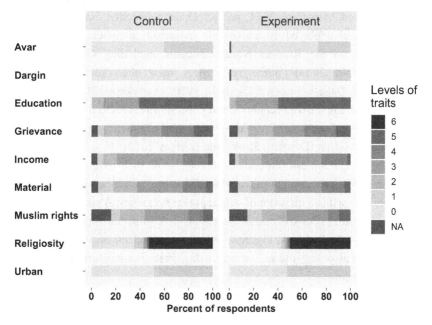

Figure 4 Distribution of demographic characteristics across treatment and control samples

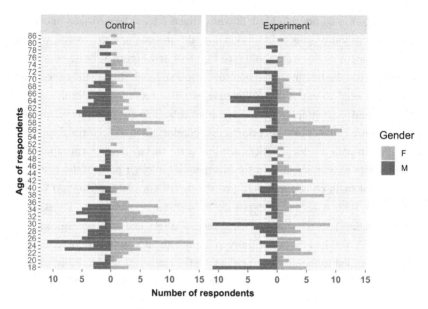

Figure 5 Age–gender pyramid

pilgrimage to the holy Muslim sites in Saudi Arabia every year. Hundreds of young people from the territory studied in Muslim institutions abroad (Ibragimov and Matsuzato 2014, p.288). Other researchers have suggested that Saudi Arabia played an active role in spreading radical Islam in its Salafist form to the Russian North Caucasus, including Chechnya and Dagestan (Gold 2004). Some researchers trace the initial spread of Wahhabism in Dagestan as far back as the 1970s (Yarlykapov 2010). Political scientists have emphasized economic and political obstacles to the functioning of secular opposition, which created conditions for channeling popular discontent through religion (Dzutsati, Siroky and Dzutsev 2016).

Since we could not ask respondents directly about their religious affiliation due to sensitivity of the religious teaching affiliation,[77] we measured religiosity of respondents with an indicator of *namaz* prayer frequency. A six-level ordinal predictor measures religiosity on an increasing scale from "no prayer at all" as 1 to "five times a day" as 6. As Figure 4 indicates, respondents mostly stated they did not pray at all or they did so five times a day, which is a standard requirement for Sunni Muslims.

---

[77] Salafism, officially referred to as Wahhabism in Dagestan, is officially outlawed according to the republican law of 1999. However, Salafi Muslim communities exist in the republic. Some of them are organized into "Salafi mosques."

Dagestan is home to dozens of ethnic groups, but only two groups alternately held on to political power after the disbandment of the USSR and up to the time of the survey implementation in 2015: Avars and Dargins. Since these two ethnic groups are the largest in the republic and play a significant role in the politics of the republic (Section 2), we include dichotomous indicators for both groups.

Education is a five-step ordinal predictor that measures the level of respondents' education from 1 as equivalent to middle school to 5 as completed a higher education degree. The majority of respondents had completed either secondary school or held a university degree. Personal income was measured as a non-monetary indicator as 1 for "income is not enough even to buy food" to 5 as "we can afford all we want." Urbanity shows whether respondents resided in a city/town or a village. About half of Dagestanis live in urban areas, with the other half being rural residents. The demographic pyramid in the sample is representative of Dagestan, with the exception of middle-aged respondents, who were underrepresented in the sample.

Figure 4 and Figure 5 display the distributions of important basic characteristics across the treatment and control samples: gender, settlement type, education, income, ethnicity, and religiosity.[78] Figure 5 compares the age pyramid between the two. The samples are well balanced for the sample size along these dimensions. It is important to assess proper balance across the two samples prior to analysis as, without it, the effects attributed to violence may in fact be due to differences across the treatment and control groups. By verifying that the two samples are similar along basic socio-demographics, we can eliminate these characteristics as confounds. If the groups are balanced, then we can be more confident in the differences of theoretical interest between the control group and the experimental group.

Now, we turn to discussion of the study's empirical results (Section 6), which analyzes the endorsements and the effects of exposure to violence on civilian support for the rebels.

6 Analysis: A Bayesian Measurement Model

This section presents and discusses the main empirical results. We find strong support for the idea that civilians' options for defection are limited and that civilians are fundamentally "hostages," compartmentalized into government and pro-insurgency camps with limited options to flee or switch to the other side. As a result, when the rebels abuse civilians, civilians tend to double down

---

[78] *Avar* and *Dargin* – the two largest ethnic groups in Dagestan – are each represented with binary (0, 1) indicators. *Urban* represents the type of settlement and is also a binary (0, 1) indicator. *Education, Income,* and *Religiosity* measure the corresponding traits on an increasing ordinal scale.

on support for their abusers; and when civilians are being victimized by the counterinsurgency, they reduce their support for the insurgency.

We also find that civilians who report *indirect* violence by the counterinsurgents express greater support for the insurgency, and civilians who report indirect insurgent violence indicate lower levels of support for the insurgency. These effects are symmetric in the sense that indirect counterinsurgent violence increases support for the insurgency, just as indirect insurgent violence reduces it. In the domain of indirect violence, unlike with directly experienced violence, we argued that civilians tend to seek out and interpret information in a way that confirms one's prior beliefs – a psychological phenomenon known as "confirmation bias" (Knobloch-Westerwick, Johnson, and Westerwick 2015; Nickerson 1998).

As a result, actors who are perceived negatively were blamed for committing indirect violence and those who were perceived positively were not deemed liable. Indirect counterinsurgent violence, based on hearsay, therefore pushed civilians further into the arms of the insurgency, where their sympathies laid anyway for the most part, whereas indirect insurgent violence pushes civilians, who are most likely already predisposed to dislike the rebels, even further away from them. This finding is also consistent with "construal level theory" in social psychology, which predicts that people use a more abstract level of perception when evaluating more temporally, spatially, and socially distant events (Liberman, Trope, and Stephan 2007; Trope and Liberman 2003).

The data indicate that there is a sharp divide between the pro-insurgency and the anti-insurgency civilian camps. Policing in each of the segments is done by their "own side" – insurgents and counterinsurgents respectively – and most violence against them is therefore highly compartmentalized. Civilians have limited opportunities for defection. Direct counterinsurgent violence thus does not push civilians into the arms of insurgency, but rather exhibits a negative effect on civilian support for the insurgency. By the same token, direct insurgent violence does not push civilians to the government side, but is instead associated with a positive effect on civilian support for insurgency. Direct violence against civilians begets loyalty.

Figure 6 provides descriptive displays of the data, illustrating the distribution of responses for the five policy questions across the control and experimental endorsement condition that were used in the subsequent analysis as the dependent variable (the full form of the policy questions is listed in the Appendix). Overall, the differences in Figure 6 (the experiments) are much larger than the socio-economic and demographic differences in Figure 4 and Figure 5. This suggests that the endorsement experiments (policies endorsed by "Forest Brothers" insurgency) cued the respondents and thereby *reduced* their support

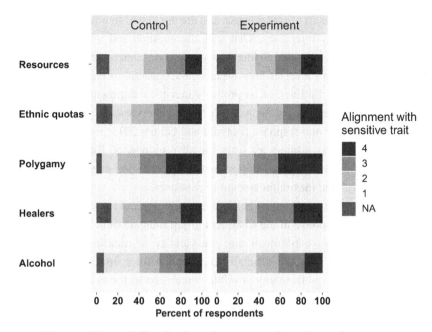

Figure 6 Overall distribution of responses from the endorsement experiments

for these policies, as expected for sensitive topics. The same effect of reduced support for given policies in experimental groups can be observed in other studies in Afghanistan and Pakistan (Bullock, Imai, and Shapiro, 2011, p. 368; Lyall, Blair, and Imai, 2013, p. 6).

The experimental condition also revealed a greater proportion of not answered (NA) responses, consistent with the sensitive nature of the subject (Figure 6). The highest non-response was observed in two of the five items: the topic of ethnic quotas and the issue of traditional healers. One might argue that the former has a higher rate of NAs because it is the most sensitive of the issues, especially for the larger ethnic groups, but the question on traditional healers has an equivalent number of NAs, and it is much less sensitive. To explore the robustness of our results, with and without these NA responses, we re-estimated the main analyses after using multiple imputation for the missing responses.[79] Although for two of the items the number of NAs in the treatment is higher, we nonetheless find that the results remain robust to several strategies for

---

[79] For multiple imputation, we utilized the R-package, Amelia II (Honaker, King and Blackwell 2011). It employs the bootstrap EM (Expectation-Maximization) algorithm to produce multiple imputed datasets; 1,000 datasets were imputed and then averaged to generate the final imputed dataset.

addressing the problem of missingness, and are not biased in a way that would alter any of the key inferences. That said, the question and interpretation of missingness, especially in conflict zones, is one that merits additional research.[80] A certain level of non-response, endogenous to the level of fear from the danger of the situation, is probably inevitable during an active insurgency and counterinsurgency campaign. Matching interviewees with interviewers can help reduce non-response (Blaydes and Gillum 2013; Benstead 2014), but it is unlikely to assuage all fears for all respondents. Researchers can complement this at the survey design and implementation stages to provide respondents with the maximum amount of reassurance.

The reduction of support for the proposed policies and the increase in the number of non-response in the treatment group indicate both the limitation of the endorsement experiment and the validity of measurement. Some respondents cued with the officially outlawed actor's opinion choose to dissociate themselves from any possible connection to the actor in order to stay personally safe. This is an understandable and sensible strategy in cases when civilians have plausible fears that they might be targeted for having an opinion about political and social phenomena. If the treatment group and the control group did not differentiate on the support for policies and non-response, it would mean that either the issue at stake does not require indirect questioning (because it is not sensitive) or that errors were made at the survey implementation stage.

Figure 7 shows the distributions of the key violence predictors: exposure to direct and indirect violence among the surveyed individuals. The number of respondents who reported exposure to indirect violence, by either rebels or counterinsurgents ("c/insurgency"), is considerably larger than the number of respondents who were affected by direct violence. This reflects a common reality in irregular wars where people are surrounded by violence but experience it directly much less frequently. It was also true in Afghanistan, where indirect violence exposure was also more common than direct violence (Lyall, Blair, and Imai 2013, p. 701).

In the case of counterinsurgent violence, for example, a district or adjacent village might be shut down. Even if a respondent was not harmed directly, in a tight-knit village or neighborhood respondents would know that something was happening and would later probably hear from someone else what happened and to whom. Finally, once we account for the non-response, more people reported experiencing *direct* violence from the insurgency than from the

---

[80] On missing data in the North Caucasus, see Naylor and O'Loughlin (2020) on patterns of non-response and how this may bias estimates for certain groups, age cohorts, regions, etc.

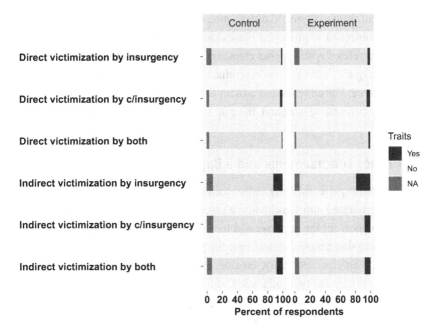

Figure 7 Overall distribution of independent variables

counterinsurgency in Dagestan, which is consistent with the expectation that rebel violence against civilians often increases after the breakdown in the "rebel rule" (Arjona 2016).[81]

A number of respondents refused to answer the question on direct violence, whether from the insurgency or counterinsurgency side, but were even more reluctant to reply when asked about direct violence from the insurgency side. The proportion of refusals to answer a question about direct insurgent violence (6.6% in control group and 6.7% in experimental group) was about twice as large as the proportion of those who refused to answer the question on being directly affected by counterinsurgency violence (3.0% and 2.3% respectively), indicating that it is riskier and more sensitive for respondents to report victimization by rebels.[82] We think it is highly likely that these refusals meant that such respondents were in fact exposed to direct violence.

---

[81] The insurgency in Dagestan rarely killed civilians, which is likely due to its critical reliance on civilian support. There are more NAs for direct victimization by the insurgency than the counterinsurgency. If we assume that these NAs are positive replies, then we can infer that the insurgency did more direct victimization than the counterinsurgency.

[82] People who were affected by counterinsurgency abuses in Dagestan frequently expressed their discontent through public protest actions, which we take as evidence that they often do not feel in danger expressing their views on this issue. On the question about direct violence by the counterinsurgency, the proportion of refusals was about the same as the proportion of those

The question on exposure to direct violence is on its own a sensitive issue that could be subject to a variety of biases. In particular, systematic missingness might be correlated with a higher chance of exposure to direct violence. If so, it is very likely that we have underestimated the amount of people exposed to direct violence. The upper bound on a revised estimate would need to include all those who refused to respond to that question and might be as high as 7 percent.[83]

6.1 Policy Endorsements and a Bayesian Measurement Model

Endorsement experiments – like other techniques discussed in earlier sections – can be incorporated into a multivariate statistical model, permitting researchers to assess support for the endorser and to simultaneously assess several alternative and complementary explanations for variation in that support. Here, we investigate ethnicity, religiosity, income, and exposure to violence, as well as controls for settlement type, education, age, and gender. The model we estimate is a Bayesian logistic regression with non-informative priors, based on the modeling technique for endorsement survey experiments developed by Bullock, Imai, and Shapiro (2011), which describes all the mechanics of the model, and is implemented in the R package "endorse."[84] Building on item response theory, this approach uses a Bayesian measurement model.

As Bullock et al. (2011, p. 369) note, this approach is essentially the same as standard ideal point models with quadratic utility functions used in political science. Parameters are added to create a model in a hierarchical fashion. The model is Bayesian, and therefore we must place prior distributions on all unknown parameters, which are usually taken to be diffuse unless strong prior knowledge of effect sizes is known from previous research or theory.

Figure 8 and Figure 9 display the main results from this model in the form of mean posterior probabilities for all individual parameters, divided by their standard deviations, along with 95% confidence intervals around them. Figure 8 shows the main results, which use the average of all five policy endorsement questions.[85]

---

who reported being indirectly affected by counterinsurgency violence. On protest in authoritarian settings, see Abbasov (2021).

[83] To the best of our knowledge, truthful answers to such questions posed no threat to respondents. Nonetheless, many people declined to respond.

[84] Bullock, Imai, and Shapiro (2011), pp. 369–372. On "endorse" in R, see Shiraito and Imai (2017).

[85] To address possible contamination for multiple endorsements, Figure 9 uses only the first policy question, discussed later in this section.

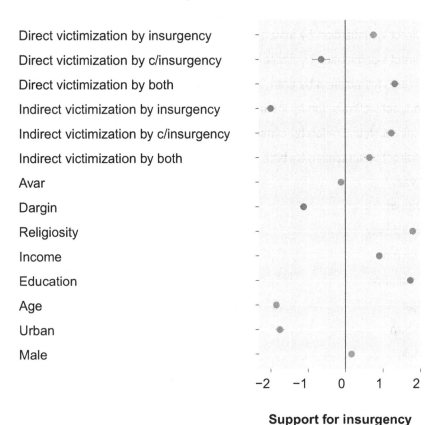

Support for insurgency

Figure 8 Bayesian logistic regression model of rebel support among civilians (coefficient plot)

Note: Dots in Figure 8 through Figure 13 represent the posterior mean effects of each predictor on support for the insurgency (displayed on the y-axis), and the lines around them are 95% confidence intervals. Following Bullock, Imai, and Shapiro (2011, 374), effects are presented in terms of standard deviations.

Civilians experiencing direct victimization at the hands of the insurgency indicated higher support for the insurgents. This finding is consistent with Hypothesis **1a**. Most civilians who already had ties to insurgents came under pressure at the time the Caucasus Emirate was transitioning into a branch of ISIS in the North Caucasus and were more likely to experience victimization. Since opportunities to switch sides to the counterinsurgency were highly limited, "defection was denied," and thus they continued to support the

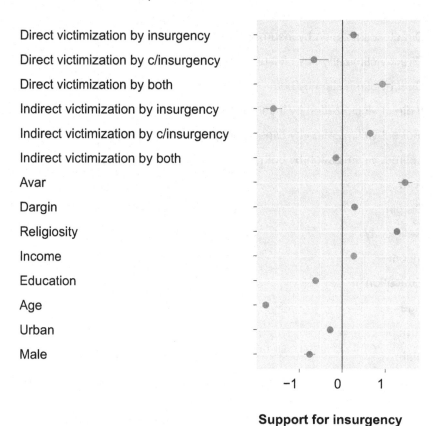

Support for insurgency

Figure 9 Coefficient plot from Bayesian logistic regression model of rebel support among civilians using first question only (resources)

insurgents. Civilians even doubled down on their support when exposed to direct insurgent violence.

Those civilians exposed to direct counterinsurgent violence did not flock to support insurgents but rather indicated lower support for them, since these were individuals already predisposed to dislike the rebels, consistent with the expectation in Hypothesis **1b**. Such civilians who experience issues with the pro-Russian government forces are on average better off facing the secular authorities than the insurgency, which is guided by Islamic law and tends to be stricter in its punishments (Lazarev 2019). Ideological attachments of course play a role: it is widely known that adherents of Salafism were more supportive of the insurgency, all else equal, whereas adherents of Sufism and agnostics tended to support the government side in Dagestan. In general, there is greater safety for civilians if they stay within their group bounds ("segments") rather than if they would aim to switch sides.

Civilians exposed to direct violence by both sides tended to express greater support for the insurgency, as specified in Hypothesis **1c**.[86] We conjecture, based on knowledge external to the survey, that this group of pro-rebel respondents could include three types of individuals: those who experienced questioning by police due to their ties with the insurgency, those caught by police for crimes unrelated to the insurgency, and those targeted by the police while his/her relative experienced direct victimization by the rebels (or vice versa). For example, a cab driver who formerly supported the Caucasus Emirate could later be approached by representatives of the new insurgency in town – IS. The same driver might have had an argument with the IS militants because, for example, he previously made a donation and performed errands for the Caucasus Emirate and now these people (very possibly the same people with different jackets!) demanded *another* payment. Independent of the cab driver's travails with the insurgents from two competing insurgent groups, he was very likely to have unfriendly encounters with the police, specifically with the traffic police, which is known for its corrupt practices in Dagestan (and elsewhere in Russia) (Oleinik 2016). This would open the taxi driver up to double victimization by insurgents and the government.

The same chain of events can be applied to people from other walks of life in Dagestan – for example, owners of small businesses and traders. Some of them may have supported insurgents and came under fire after the change of hands in the insurgency. At the same time, based on the nature of their occupations, they were very likely to have unfriendly encounters with the police.[87]

---

[86] When only the first of five questions was used to estimate the model (Figure 9), direct victimization by both sides was not statistically significant.

[87] For example, in some model specifications, direct victimization by both sides is only marginally and positively correlated with support for insurgents (Figure 12), while in others it is robustly and positively correlated with support for insurgents (Figure 8, Figure 9, and Figure 13).

Victims react in a way that they think will keep them and their families safer, and conditional upon their ability to defect. Direct and indirect exposure to violence lead to different risk assessments and disparate solutions. If the Islamic insurgency directly inflicted violence on the respondent or their immediate family, such civilians are likely to have few (if any) alternatives. They cannot go to the counterinsurgency for protection, and they cannot emigrate, so (along the lines of the hostage logic) they determine that their safety actually lies deeper in the arms of the insurgency.[88] Given their social and economic dependency on local ethnic clan networks, victimized civilians embrace their abusers.

When it comes to indirect violence, compared to those of direct violence, we find that the effects are reversed. Unlike direct violence, civilians exposed to indirect insurgent violence were *less* likely to express support for the rebels, and civilians who heard of counterinsurgent violence were *more* likely to support the insurgents, consistent with Hypothesis **2a**. In other words, whereas direct violence by the rebels did not push civilians away from the insurgency, hearing about insurgent violence reduced civilian support for rebels. Hearing about counterinsurgency violence increased support for the insurgency, consistent with Hypothesis **2b**.

We also find that those who have been exposed to indirect violence by both sides were slightly more likely to support the insurgency, but the effect was not statistically significant across all model specifications, and under some model specifications the mean estimate was negatively correlated with the support for insurgency, which casts doubt on Hypothesis **2c** (cf. Figure 8, Figure 9 and Figure 12). The discrepancy between the effects, we suspect, concerns the different mechanisms at play with direct and indirect victimization. *Whereas direct violence is connected to costly personal experiences and an inability to defect, indirect violence is about opinions, values, and confirmation bias.*

We also provide data analysis with imputed missing values (Figure 10).[89] Results of the analysis of imputed data are very close to the main analysis. In line with expectations, direct victimization of respondents by insurgency is associated with their higher support for insurgents, just as direct victimization of respondents by the

---

[88] One loophole allowed some Wahabis to join the Hijra, which the FSB allegedly supported for some unknown time window in 2015.

[89] Imputed values with decimal points in hypothesis variables measuring direct and indirect victimization by the insurgency and counterinsurgency were rounded to 0, if <0.5 and 1, if >=0.5.

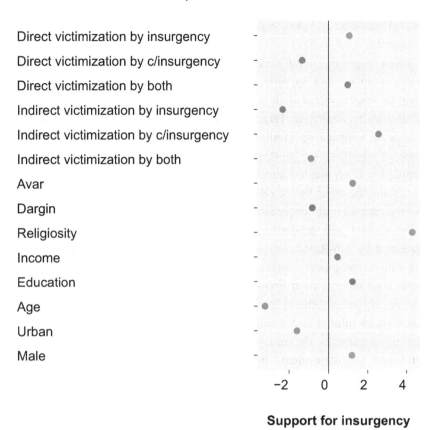

Support for insurgency

Figure 10 Coefficient plot from Bayesian logistic regression model (with multiple imputation)

counterinsurgency is associated with their lower support for insurgents. The relationship is reversed for indirect victimization. Indirect victimization by the insurgency is associated with lower support for insurgents among respondents, just as indirect victimization by the counterinsurgency is associated with higher support for insurgents.

It seems that insurgents have a home advantage, as respondents who are directly victimized by both sides tend to increase their support the insurgency. The only significant difference between the main analysis and supplemental analysis of imputed data is that ethnic Avars appear to be on average more supportive of the insurgency than other ethnic groups.[90] Indirect victimization

---

[90] Since Avars gained access to official power in Dagestan prior to the survey, we expected that they would be less supportive of the insurgency, which they are in some specifications but not in all. This is an issue for further investigation.

by neither side is associated with marginally greater support for the insurgents.

Taken together, these findings make it clear that *the influence of violence on civilian support for the insurgency thus depends not only upon its source, but also on the type of exposure to violence and the lack of options to defect.* In Dagestan, we interpret these results about the effects of violence on civilian support as evidence consistent with the view of civilians as "hostages" to the warring parties. The civilian population is segmented into two groups: one ruled by the counterinsurgency and the other by the rebels. Civilians affiliated with the insurgency mostly interact with insurgents. This sorting shapes response to violence, since secular and moderate Muslim civilians are more likely to be governed by pro-Russian rulers, and religious civilians are subjected to the rule of religiously infused rebels. Both groups are more likely to experience victimization from their own rulers. This effect is likely to be particularly robust among rural inhabitants and insurgents, where clan-based socio-cultural codes and controls are known to be strongest. Being directly targeted by the insurgents does not imply, as it might in a more fluid and less dependent situation, that one reduces support for the insurgency – on the contrary, those targeted directly by the insurgency are *more* likely to support the insurgency. Despite lacking territorial control, the rebels were nonetheless capable of exercising a degree of control over civilians, partly as a result of strong socio-cultural codes, clientelistic dependency, and security protection that operate through clans and ethnicity (Kisriev and Ware 2006).

We also examine the role of several threats to inference. First, we assess the possibility of learning on the part of respondents after they were exposed to the first question, since we used a set of five questions with endorsers. If respondents "learn" about the survey technique after the initial endorser, they would answer the subsequent questions in a biased way (Eriksen 1960; Romeo and Sopher 1999; Savage and Waldman 2008). While there is a potential risk of the learning effect, and contamination that may result, multiple endorsement questions are a safer choice for researchers because not all available policies are equally well known and important for respondents. Having several treatments allowed us to account for variations in preferences and prior knowledge of existing policy choices. We could also isolate the effect of the endorser caused by respondents' support for the insurgency as opposed to other factors.

We nonetheless test for this possibility by analyzing only the first endorsement experiment (resources), and excluding the following four. Figure 9 displays the results of the analysis. Respondents who experienced direct victimization by the insurgency were more likely to support it, whereas respondents who experienced direct victimization by the counter-insurgency were less likely to support the insurgency. Direct victimization by both sides increased civilian support for the insurgency in the main model (Figure 8), however, but not in a specification where only the first of five questions was used (Figure 9). We conjecture that the discrepancy is likely related to the diversity of individuals affected by both types of violence (wide intervals on the point estimates) and also possibly due to the loss of statistical power.

The relationship between support for insurgents and *indirect* victimization is also similar to the main analysis. Respondents who recollect violence by insurgents in their neighborhood were less likely to support the insurgency, while respondents who remembered violence by counter-insurgents near their home were more likely to support the insurgency. Respondents who were indirectly victimized by both tended to lower their support for the insurgency. This latter indicator is not statistically significant, which cuts against the expectations laid out in Hypothesis **2c**, and is likely due to the inherent heterogeneity of the group that has been exposed indirectly to both insurgency and counterinsurgency violence. This is not entirely surprising since the effect was not that strong even with all of the power provided by the experiments combined.

Next, we investigate the possible role of ethnicity, which could have many effects in Dagestan. We consider a major ethnic cleavage between the largest two groups and the others, which allows us to assess whether being Avar or Dargin (the two largest ethnicities) was positively correlated with support for the insurgency, which was ruled by each of the groups sequentially.[91] The results indicate that, all else equal, Dargins were some-what less likely to support the insurgency than Avars and all other groups in Dagestan (such as Kumyks, Avars, Lezgins, or Azeris; cf. Figure 11 and Figure 12). Dargins did not appear to be particularly supportive of the insurgency, despite the fact that they (Magomedsalam Magomedov, a Dargin governor of Dagestan) lost secular power in January 2013 to Avars (Ramazan Abdulatipov, an Avar). Avars were on average slightly more supportive of the insurgency than other ethnic groups even though an

---

[91] Russian Census in Dagestan (2010): Avars 29%, Dargin 17%, Kumyk 15%, Lezgin 13%, Laks 6%, other groups are less than 5%.

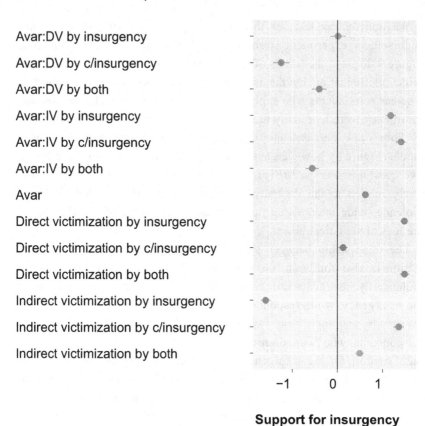

Support for insurgency

Figure 11 Coefficient plot from Bayesian logistic regression model (interaction: Avar *x* violence)

ethnic Avar ruled Dagestan at the time of the survey. (see Figure 10). This may have reflected the fact that Dagestani Avars at the time – successively, Aliaskhab Kebekov in 2014–2015 and Magomed Suleimanov in 2015 – were in charge of the Caucasus Emirate and enjoyed greater support among their ethnic kin.

We have discussed religion throughout the manuscript. When we asked about *namaz*, we found that religiosity was positively associated with support for the insurgency. This is not surprising given the strong religious overtones in the conflict and the insurgencies association with Salafi Islam in Dagestan. We also assessed economic, geographic, and demographic factors. We found that wealthier, younger, more educated, male respondents were all more likely to support the rebels, all else

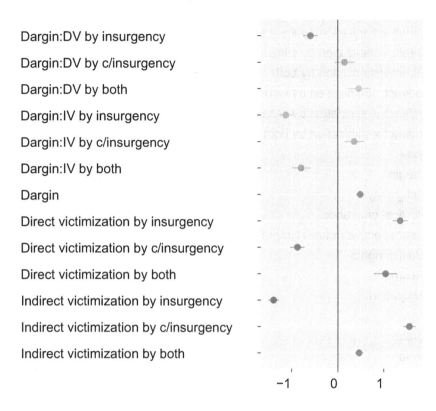

Dargin:DV by insurgency
Dargin:DV by c/insurgency
Dargin:DV by both
Dargin:IV by insurgency
Dargin:IV by c/insurgency
Dargin:IV by both
Dargin
Direct victimization by insurgency
Direct victimization by c/insurgency
Direct victimization by both
Indirect victimization by insurgency
Indirect victimization by c/insurgency
Indirect victimization by both

−1   0   1

Support for insurgency

Figure 12 Coefficient plot from Bayesian logistic regression model
(interaction: violence *x* Dargin)

equal; yet so were more rural folks, who are generally poorer, older, and less educated.

Those who expressed positive retrospective economic evaluations were associated with less support for the rebels, and those who think that the central authorities of Russia (in Moscow) are not solving Dagestan's problems – and have not protected the rights of Muslims – were more likely to support the rebels. The inclusion and exclusion of these factors did not alter any of the main results, and the findings that exposure to violence has strong effects on civilian support for the insurgency remains robust.

6.2 Comparing Dagestan and Afghanistan

In Section 2, we discussed the differences and similarities in initial conditions with some other cases, most notably Afghanistan. Now, we are in a better position to

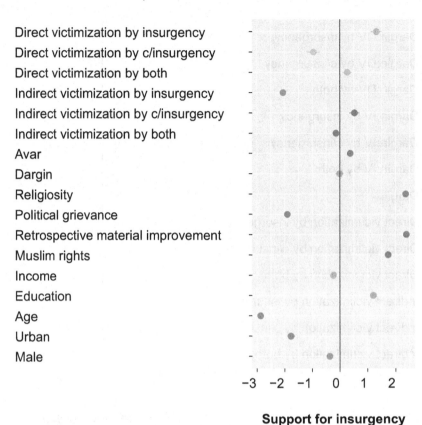

Direct victimization by insurgency
Direct victimization by c/insurgency
Direct victimization by both
Indirect victimization by insurgency
Indirect victimization by c/insurgency
Indirect victimization by both
Avar
Dargin
Religiosity
Political grievance
Retrospective material improvement
Muslim rights
Income
Education
Age
Urban
Male

−3 −2 −1   0   1   2

Support for insurgency

Figure 13 Coefficient plot from Bayesian logistic regression model (additional covariates)

compare results. Field and survey experiments conducted in single countries should try to evaluate the extent to which their findings are likely to generalize to other settings and how they compare with other micro-level studies. Although the levels of support for militancy will naturally vary across contexts, the processes and relationships studied here may generalize to similar settings and contexts, subject to comparable scope conditions. The existence of comparable studies, aiming to study the civilian support base of rebel organizations in countries such as Afghanistan, Iraq, and Pakistan (e.g., Berman, Shapiro, and Felter 2011; Blair, Fair, Malhotra, and Shapiro 2013; Blair and Imai 2012; Bullock, Imai, and Shapiro 2011; Lyall, Blair, and Imai 2013), provides an important baseline against which to compare the inferences made about civilian support in this study. Such comparisons allow us to establish the extent to which these processes and relationships travel across different regions and settings; and, equally as crucial, why some results may differ across contexts.

Just as in Afghanistan (e.g., Lyall, Blair, and Imai 2013), when the insurgents harmed individuals directly in Dagestan, civilians boosted support for them. We also find an asymmetric effect in Dagestan that is similar to Afghanistan. When civilians are affected by both insurgency and counterinsurgency, they side with the insurgency, which also speaks to a certain bias in favor of the insurgency, although one that is much smaller than in Afghanistan. However, where direct victimization by Western ISAF increased Taliban support, pushing civilians into the arms of the rebels, direct victimization by Russia's counterinsurgency forces *reduced* support for the rebels in Dagestan, reflecting the compartmentalization of violence and the lack of defection options in Dagestan.

Another important finding emerges from the comparison with Afghanistan, where the effects of direct and indirect violence are similar across individual and *manteqa* (zone) levels. The difference between the effects of direct and indirect violence on civilian support in Afghanistan is one of magnitude: the estimated effects on support levels for each combatant are diminished at the *manteqa* level, especially for ISAF, "when there is indirect violence" (Lyall, Blair, and Imai 2013, 692). In Dagestan, as we theorized earlier, we do not see indirect violence as simply a weaker form of direct violence, but rather as a qualitatively distinct experience. It is mostly driven by confirmation bias – namely, attributing negative events and information to the "other" and positive events and information to "one's own side" (Knobloch-Westerwick, Johnson, and Westerwick 2015; Nickerson 1998). As a result, in Dagestan, we find that the effects of direct and indirect violence are not just diminished with "distance from the violence," but run in the opposite direction, consistent with this psychological understanding of indirect violence.

We also wish to highlight several factors that might shed further light on these differences. First, when we think of the counterinsurgency and their commitment, it is very clear that the USA and ISAF were significantly less committed to instilling law and order in the whole territory of Afghanistan, which remained a foreign land where there were no plans for long-term settlement. For Russia, Dagestan was and is an integral part of its territory, one that had to be pacified by almost any means for the sake of the entire country. Russia has longer time horizons in Dagestan than Western troops in Afghanistan, and elsewhere outside the homeland.

Second, Russia's regime type and human rights record – compared to the rules by which ISAF were operating in Afghanistan – allowed it to impose heavy penalties on citizens who expressed any support for insurgents, something ISAF could never do in Afghanistan for civilians who supported the Taliban. This has enabled Russian authorities to brush aside concerns about civil liberties and reconciliation processes, and to kill off almost any number of insurgents, their relatives, and their civilian support base. Unlike ISAF, which sought to flip rebels to their side, Russia has completely blocked the potential rehabilitation of those who might wish to change sides, denying defection and leaving insurgents with no option but to keep fighting. This policy has created a sharp divide among civilians between those who support the insurgency and the rest of the population.

The counterinsurgency's "narrow valve" allowed civilians to temporarily move in only one direction – from the pro-government camp to the insurgency camp, but not the other way around. This was not an attractive option since defection implied a loss of local ties, support, and protection. In fact, most secular Dagestanis do not wish to join the insurgency – and many could not, even if they did wish to join it. Civilians are in effect in a state of capture by the rebel or the counterinsurgency camps, and have sided accordingly, often *despite* exposure to direct violence.

Third, culture matters. Due to the long history of coexistence and acculturation to Russian language and lifestyle, a considerable pro-secular and pro-Russian segment of the population existed in Dagestan prior to the recent conflict. The cultural distance between Russians and Dagestanis is much smaller than the cultural difference between the US/ISAF and Afghanis. The counterinsurgency in Dagestan was not completely an "out-group" for all Dagestanis, which meant greater support for it on the ground and less mobilization against it. Whereas there is a cultural difference between Dagestani Salafis and Sufis and ethnic Russians, the former two are still ethnic Dagestanis, and all three of these groups speak a common language. The cultural and linguistic distance between US/ISAF soldiers and local Afghanis exceeds the cultural distance in Dagestan by a large margin. Due to a long period of coexistence, a large proportion of the population in Dagestan is assimilated or at least accultured to life in Russia (e.g., Russian language proficiency and exposure to Russian media), rendering the in-group and out-group distinction less clear and more fluid than in Afghanistan between ISAF and the Taliban.[92]

Further comparisons would of course be welcome and would enhance our ability to assess the extent to which these results generalize to other times and contexts. After a collection of such studies have been published, we will be in a stronger position to determine the relative importance of various factors, how they interact with and depend upon contextual features, and how to best go about crafting a general understanding of civilian attitudes toward militant groups in irregular wars.

---

[92] Some practical consequences of these differences include widespread Christian proselytism in Dagestan and the near absence of it in Afghanistan.

While the survey is agnostic about cultural factors, it seems clear that contextual factors are needed for a credible interpretation, and even for the effective design of experiments. Quantitative analysis inevitably ignores a great deal of relevant contextual information for the sake of standardization and comparability. The recommendation in the literature is therefore to account for non-quantifiable factors that might influence the outcomes (Seawright 2021, p. 387). For example, consider power. While ISAF in Afghanistan potentially might be just as strong vis-à-vis the Taliban as the Russian forces were vis-à-vis Dagestani insurgents, comparing raw military or economic power often does little justice to the actual story on the ground. The relative resolve of the insurgency and counterinsurgency is a key factor, as this is in part a function of the time horizons we discussed earlier. As we know from Afghanistan and Iraq, and many other "small wars," counterinsurgencies vary in the degree to which they are committed in the long term. Dagestan is politically a part of the Russian Federation, and hence the central government has a legitimate claim to establishing control over the territory and to a monopoly on the use of force.

Likewise, the cultural affinities between the sides in the conflict that we also discussed are not well captured in the survey or the results. The fact that Russians and Dagestanis share many cultural norms, speak the same language, and have lived side by side for years played a large role in ensuring that a substantial part of the population supported the counterinsurgency in Dagestan, regardless of its abuses, which was much less the case in Afghanistan. A significant part of the population in Dagestan does not adhere to basic Islamic canons and behavior, and some even converted to various Christian denominations – something unheard of and punishable in Afghanistan.[93] Navigating the diversity of religious and ethnic affiliations and territorially grounded clan-based structures and alliances requires attention to context and societal trends, which are not always quantifiable either by their nature or due to lack of reliable data.

Finally, at the time of our survey, the insurgency movement was in the midst of transforming from a local rebellion into a branch of an international jihadi franchise. The homegrown Caucasus Emirate in Dagestan evolved into an arm of ISIS, which we presume reduced the level of support for the rebels (but alas, our survey cannot disentangle this, since it was not anticipated). During this process, loyalties within the insurgency movement and its civilian support base were being rewritten and rewired. These experiments therefore captured an important moment in the

---

[93] Conversions have gone in both directions, with many ethnic Russian converts to Islam in Dagestan (one of them killed the chief mufti of Dagestan in a suicide attack in 2012).

evolution of an irregular war, one that we did not anticipate and that would be therefore nearly impossible to repeat with any predictability.

7 Conclusion

Why do civilians fall into the arms of abusive insurgents? Using indirect questioning techniques in Dagestan, this Element argues that sticky identities, economic dependency, and security concerns curb the ability of civilians to switch loyalties. Since "defection is denied" and civilian attitudes follow from the societal lock-in, direct victimization increases support for the perpetrators of violence.

Whereas most research has focused on the armed actors and the causes of violence against civilians, this study investigates the correlates of wartime attitudes toward an insurgency. We engage with the use of indirect questioning techniques, and specifically endorsement experiments, for sensitive topics in dangerous settings: situations in which asking questions directly is not optimal or sometimes feasible. We discuss the design, implementation, and interpretation of a specific study about civilians, rebels, and counterinsurgents in an authoritarian. We conducted the study in a region where this has never been done before, and in a type of a homegrown civil war that is common but has not yet been analyzed using unobtrusive experimental methods.

Following in the footsteps of previous researchers, we distinguish between the *sources* of violence (insurgency/counterinsurgency) and *type* of exposure to violence (direct/indirect). Specifically, we explore the effect of civilian exposure to direct and indirect violence at the hands of the insurgency and the counterinsurgency on civilian support for the insurgency. We argue that, in Dagestan, the ability of civilians to defect is limited due to their embeddedness in territorially defined clans, sticky identities, and dependence on ethnic favoritism. Civilians are effectively "hostages" that are compartmentalized into pro-government and pro-insurgency "segments" with limited options to flee and switch sides. As a result, when the rebels abuse civilians, civilians tend to double down on their support for the insurgency rather than reduce it. When civilians were victimized by the counterinsurgency, it had the reverse effect of reducing support for the insurgency, since these were mostly already anti-insurgent civilians, just as those targeted by the rebels were mostly pro-rebel civilians. Finally, some unfortunate civilians were exposed to the direct violence from *both* sides, and these individuals displayed attitudes that favored the insurgency.

Exposure to indirect violence is qualitatively distinct. We find that the effects of violence are reversed when civilians "hear" about it (indirect violence) compared to when they experience it firsthand. Civilians who report indirect violence (based on hearsay) by the counterinsurgents express *more* support for the insurgency, and civilians who report indirect insurgent violence express *less* support for the insurgency. These effects are symmetric in that indirect counterinsurgent violence increases support for the insurgency just as indirect insurgent violence reduces it. We attribute the effect of indirect violence on civilian support for insurgency to "confirmation bias." When respondents hear that the opposing side abused civilians, it solidifies the preconception that the opposing side combatants are bad and the rumor therefore increases support for the respondents' own side.

This Element combines experimental design with area expertise, domain knowledge, and qualitative research, which we have argued are all indispensable not only for designing experimental research but also for interpreting results effectively. Knowing and exploiting structural and temporal factors of interest can be crucial for understanding complex social phenomena. Regime type, relative power of warring factions, disparate time horizons, and splinter movements can significantly shape the calculus of state and non-state actors. This context provides important cues for understanding the undercurrents in conflict-ridden societies, and is crucial to properly designing and interpreting experimental studies, particularly (but of course not exclusively) those in dangerous settings.

Reducing violence requires a deeper understanding of the underlying forces that shape actor motivations and mobilization capacity, along with communications and operations in irregular wars. This Element advances our understanding of the role of civilians in insurgency by clarifying how civilian victimization via direct and indirect violence shapes individual support for insurgent groups. In this way, it sheds new light on the interaction of civilians' loyalties, violence, and insurgency in irregular wars. Acquiring reliable data during an ongoing civil conflict is always a challenge. This Element provides both a theoretical and a practical overview of some ways to deal with this challenge.

The Element's approach can be extended, for instance, to study the correlates of civilian support for other non-state actors – ranging from fringe social movements to volunteer home-guard groups – or to investigate the determinants of transitions from passive to more active forms of support, including the drivers of radicalization and deradicalization. The finding that direct violence instills compliance among civilians points to the rather grim implication that the most successful way to lock-in civilian support may be to terrorize and eliminate the possibility of defection for insurgency supporters. Such policies, however, are unlikely to succeed unless the target population is locally dependent on ethnic or other sticky ties for material support and physical safety, Furthermore, the logic of "defection denied" is particularly relevant in situations where civilians are integrated into the nation's life, the insurgency is relatively weak, and the government is able to divert attention – and avoid domestic criticism – using brutal counterinsurgency methods.

Recent developments around the world highlight the need for an improved understanding of the role of civilians in insurgencies and group mobilization. The project's rigorous examination of how exposure to violence shapes beliefs and attitudes toward an insurgency has national security implications, especially for the design of counterinsurgency and counterterrorism strategies. The Element underscores some general principles that could, with appropriate modification, potentially apply to other insurgencies, and can help us to better understand the sources of civilian support for insurgents in tomorrow's irregular wars. In this way, social science can help inform policymaking on crucial problems of the day.

This Element is about understanding irregular wars, and the interaction of civilians, violence, and insurgency within them. More generally, it shows how social scientists can ethically, prudently, and effectively utilize experimental methods to gain analytical leverage to study sensitive social, political, and security topics that could put respondents, researchers, and enumerators at risk in war zones. By engaging in a critical discussion of available techniques for the elicitation of truthful responses to sensitive issues, and by providing guidelines on how to integrate qualitative research into experimental research through an application to an important but dangerous area of social science inquiry, this Element hopefully offers some encouragement for researchers who could benefit from using these unobtrusive techniques in their own sensitive research across a wide range of dangerous settings.

Appendix

Table 1A Descriptive statistics for control group

variable	n	missing, %	mean	sd	median	min	max	skew	kurtosis	se
Resources	267	11.88	2.80	1.12	3	1	4	−0.37	−1.27	0.07
Ethnic quotas	258	14.85	2.60	1.09	3	1	4	−0.11	−1.30	0.07
Polygamy	288	4.95	2.17	1.09	2	1	4	0.38	−1.19	0.06
Healers	261	13.86	2.21	0.94	2	1	4	0.46	−0.65	0.06
Alcohol	282	6.93	2.75	1.13	3	1	4	−0.24	−1.37	0.07
Direct violence by insurgency	283	6.60	0.03	0.17	0	0	1	5.66	30.17	0.01
Direct violence by c/insurgency	294	2.97	0.04	0.21	0	0	1	4.41	17.52	0.01
Indirect violence by insurgency	280	7.59	0.24	0.43	0	0	1	1.24	−0.47	0.03
Indirect violence by c/insurgency	277	8.58	0.23	0.42	0	0	1	1.27	−0.39	0.03
Muslim rights	254	16.17	2.93	1.06	3	1	5	0.21	−0.31	0.07
Retrospective material improve	287	5.28	2.84	1.08	3	1	5	−0.05	−0.57	0.06
Political grievance	288	4.95	3.28	1.15	3	1	5	−0.12	−0.91	0.07
Age	303	0.00	43.85	18.19	36	18	86	0.32	−1.38	1.05

Male	303	0.00	0.47	0.50	0	1	0.11	-1.99	0.03
Education	303	0.00	4.12	1.13	5	5	-0.67	-1.18	0.07
Income	289	4.62	3.08	0.84	3	5	-0.25	0.68	0.05
Urban	303	0.00	0.49	0.50	0	1	0.06	-2.00	0.03
Avar	303	0.00	0.41	0.49	0	1	0.38	-1.86	0.03
Dargin	303	0.00	0.11	0.32	0	1	2.45	3.99	0.02
Prayer	303	0.00	3.41	2.85	6	6	-0.25	-1.88	0.16

Table 2A Descriptive statistics for experimental group

variable	n	missing, %	mean	sd	median	min	max	skew	kurtosis	se
Resources	246	17.73	2.44	1.09	2	1	4	0.11	−1.30	0.07
Ethnic quotas	236	21.07	2.51	1.10	2	1	4	0.06	−1.33	0.07
Polygamy	271	9.36	1.96	1.07	2	1	4	0.74	−0.80	0.07
Healers	242	19.06	2.00	0.93	2	1	4	0.73	−0.29	0.06
Alcohol	267	10.70	2.65	1.10	3	1	4	−0.12	−1.33	0.07
Direct violence by insurgency	279	6.69	0.07	0.25	0	0	1	3.41	9.67	0.02
Direct violence by c/insurgency	292	2.34	0.08	0.27	0	0	1	3.11	7.71	0.02
Indirect violence by insurgency	279	6.69	0.29	0.46	0	0	1	0.90	−1.19	0.03
Indirect violence by c/ insurgency	280	6.35	0.18	0.38	0	0	1	1.67	0.79	0.02
Muslim rights	255	14.72	2.80	1.15	3	1	5	0.26	−0.50	0.07
Retrospective material improve	278	7.02	2.87	1.04	3	1	5	−0.07	−0.46	0.06
Political grievance	279	6.69	3.13	1.18	3	1	5	−0.11	−0.89	0.07
Age	299	0.00	44.67	16.99	42	18	82	0.06	−1.24	0.98

Male	299	0.00	0.48	0.50	0	1	0.06	−2.00	0.03
Education	299	0.00	4.15	1.06	5	2	−0.55	−1.44	0.06
Income	285	4.68	3.02	0.81	3	1	−0.08	0.17	0.05
Urban	299	0.00	0.52	0.50	1	0	−0.09	−2.00	0.03
Avar	295	1.34	0.28	0.45	0	0	0.99	−1.03	0.03
Dargin	295	1.34	0.15	0.35	0	0	2.00	2.00	0.02
Prayer	299	0.00	3.17	2.92	5	6	−0.10	−1.95	0.17

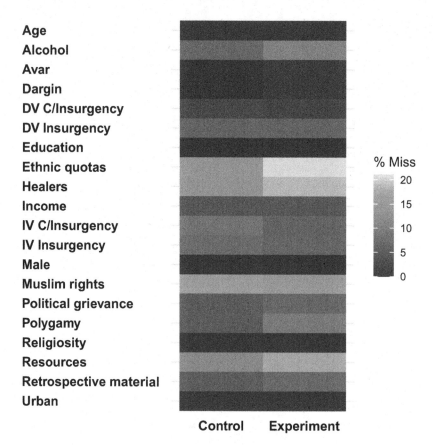

Figure 1A Missingness map

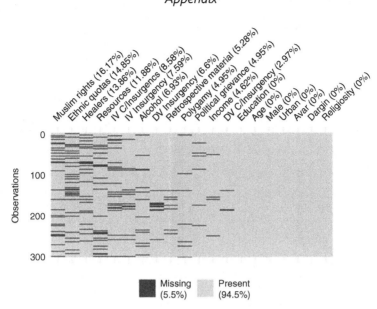

Figure 2A Missingness map: control group

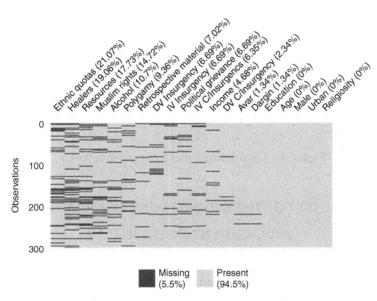

Figure 3A Missingness map: experimental group

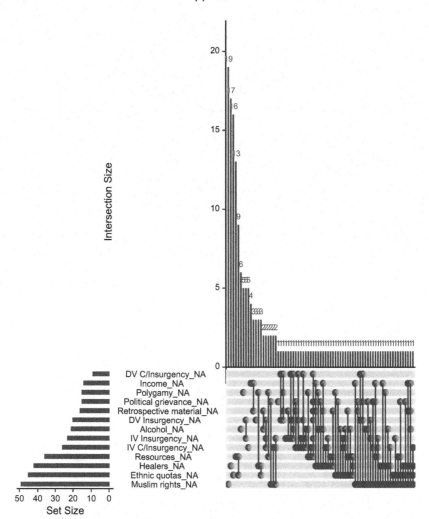

Figure 4A Missingness correlations: control group

FULL TEXT OF THE ENDORSEMENT EXPERIMENTS

ENDORSEMENT EXPERIMENT 1

Policy Issue 1 – Energy

Endorsement treatment condition (random 50% of respondents)

Q. Dagestan has significant energy resources, but they are not under republican control. *The "Forest Brothers"* think that if Dagestan were allowed to take control of its natural resources, it could help the republic develop economically. What do you think?

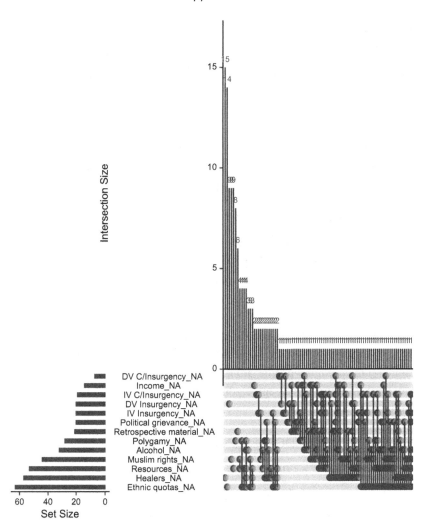

Figure 5A Missingness correlations: experimental group

1) Strongly agree
2) Agree
3) Disagree
4) Strongly disagree
5) No Opinion

Control condition (random 50% of respondents)

Q. Dagestan has significant energy resources, but they are not under republican control. Some people think that if Dagestan were allowed to take control of its natural resources, it could help the republic develop economically. What do you think?

1) Strongly agree
2) Agree
3) Disagree
4) Strongly disagree
5) No Opinion

ENDORSEMENT EXPERIMENT 2

Policy Issue 2 – Government Jobs and Ethnic Quotas

Treatment (random 50% of respondents)

Q. Government jobs in Dagestan are often distributed according to ethnic quotas. *The "Forest Brothers"* think that this is wrong. Would you say that you strongly agree, agree, disagree, strongly disagree, or have no opinion?

Control (random 50% of respondents)

Q. Government jobs in Dagestan are often distributed according to ethnic quotas. Some people think that this is wrong. Would you say that you strongly agree, agree, disagree, strongly disagree, or have no opinion?

ENDORSEMENT EXPERIMENT 3

Policy Issue 3 – Monogamy

Treatment (random 50% of respondents)

Q. Monogamy (having only one spouse) is the rule in contemporary Russia. *The "Forest Brothers"* say, however, that allowing men to have several wives would solve some demographic issues. Would you say that you strongly agree, agree, disagree, strongly disagree, or have no opinion?

Control (random 50% of respondents)

Q. Monogamy (having only one spouse) is the rule in contemporary Russia. Some people say, however, that allowing men to have several wives would solve some demographic issues. Would you say that you strongly agree, agree, disagree, strongly disagree, or have no opinion?

ENDORSEMENT EXPERIMENT 4

Policy Issue 4 – Healers

Treatment (random 50% of respondents)

Q. Many people turn to healers that use potions to heal people. *The "Forest Brothers,"* however, say that these practices should be outlawed and punished. Would you say that you strongly agree, agree, disagree, strongly disagree, or have no opinion?

Control (random 50% of respondents)

Q. Many people turn to healers that use potions to heal people. Some people say, however, that these practices should be outlawed and punished. Would you say that you strongly agree, agree, disagree, strongly disagree, or have no opinion?

ENDORSEMENT EXPERIMENT 5

Policy Issue 5 – Alcohol Tax

Treatment (random 50% of respondents)

Q. Alcohol factories bring a considerable amount of money into the budget in Dagestan. *The "Forest Brothers"* say, however, that it's immoral to make money on selling alcohol. Would you say that you strongly agree, agree, disagree, strongly disagree, or have no opinion?

Control (random 50% of respondents)

Q. Alcohol factories bring a considerable amount of money into the budget in Dagestan. Some people say, however, that it's immoral to make money on selling alcohol. Would you say that you strongly agree, agree, disagree, strongly disagree, or have no opinion?

Coding and recoding of endorsement questions

Original value	#	Recoded value[1]	#
Strongly agree	1	Strongly agree	4
Agree	2	Agree	3
Disagree	3	Disagree	2
Strongly disagree	4	Strongly disagree	1
Hard to say	5	NA	-

---

[1] Responses to the question in survey experiment 2 on ethnic quotas were recoded the opposite way (i.e., along the lines of the original coding), since "Forest Brothers" were ideologically opposed to emphasizing ethnic differences.

HYPOTHESIS-RELATED QUESTIONS

In the past year, have you or any of your family physically suffered as the result of militants' actions?

Original value	#	Recoded value	#
Yes	1	Yes	1
No	2	No	0
Hard to say	3	Yes	1

In the past year, have you or any of your family physically suffered as the result of law enforcement agents' actions?

Original value	#	Recoded value	#
Yes	1	Yes	1
No	2	No	0
Hard to say	3	Yes	1

In the past year, have you heard of anyone in your village/city who physically suffered as the result of militants' actions?

Original value	#	Recoded value	#
Yes	1	Yes	1
No	2	No	0
Hard to say	3	NA	-

In the past year, have you heard of anyone in your village/city who physically suffered as the result of law enforcement agents' actions?

Original value	#	Recoded value	#
Yes	1	Yes	1
No	2	No	0
Hard to say	3	NA	-

CODING AND WORDING FOR OTHER VARIABLES

How well do the Russian authorities protect the rights of fellow Muslim citizens?

Original value	#	Recoded value	#
Very well	1	Very well	1
Fairly well	2	Fairly well	2
Neither well nor badly	3	Neither well nor badly	3
Fairly badly	4	Fairly badly	4
Very badly	5	Very badly	5
Hard to say	6	NA	-

Do you think there have been changes in your personal financial situation over the last year? Has it improved or worsened?

Original value	#	Recoded value	#
It has deteriorated considerably	1	It has deteriorated considerably	1
It's gotten a little worse	2	It's gotten a little worse	2
It's about the same as before	3	It's about the same as before	3
It's improved a little	4	It's improved a little	4
It's improved considerably	5	It's improved considerably	5
Hard to say	6	NA	-

How satisfied are you with the way the Russian government copes with regional problems?

Original value	#	Recoded value	#
Very satisfied	1	Very satisfied	1
Rather satisfied	2	Rather satisfied	2
Neither satisfied nor dissatisfied	3	Neither satisfied nor dissatisfied	3
Rather dissatisfied	4	Rather dissatisfied	4
Very dissatisfied	5	Very dissatisfied	5
Hard to say	6	NA	-

Speaking of your financial situation, which of the following population groups do you belong to?

Original value	#	Recoded value	#
We don't even have enough money to buy food	1	We don't even have enough money to buy food	1
We have enough money for food, but not for clothes	2	We have enough money for food, but not for clothes	2
We have enough money for food and clothes	3	We have enough money for food and clothes	3
Sometimes we can afford to buy expensive things	4	Sometimes we can afford to buy expensive things	4
We can afford everything	5	We can afford everything	5
Hard to say	6	NA	-

Do you do namaz? (daily prayer)

1. Yes -> How many times?
2. No -> 0

How many times a day on average?

Original value	#	Recoded value	#
Once a day	1	Once a day	2
Twice a day	2	Twice a day	3
Thrice a day	3	Thrice a day	4
Four times a day	4	Four times a day	5
Five times a day	5	Five times a day	6
From time to time	6	From time to time	1
Not at all	-	Not at all	0

Dichotomous indicators: Male, Urban, Avar, Dargin. Age of respondents divided by 10.

Author Biographies

David S. Siroky studies cooperation, conflict and collective action in politics and economics, an is also engaged in research on social science research methodology. He is Professor of Government at the University of Essex. More information at www.davidsiroky.com.

Valery Dzutsati is Visiting Assistant Professor at the University of Kansas. His research focuses on civil violence, politics and religion, and democratization.

Lenka Bustikova is Associate Professor of European Union and Comparative East European Politics at the University of Oxford. Her book, *Extreme Reactions: Radical Right Mobilization in Eastern Europe* (Cambridge University Press), received Harvard University's Davis Center Book Prize in political and social studies awarded by the Association for Slavic, East European, and Eurasian Studies (2020).

References

Abadie, A. 2006. "Poverty, Political Freedom, and the Roots of Terrorism." *American Economic Review*, 96(2), 50–56.

Abbasov, N. 2021. "Antigovernment Protests and Commitment to Democratic Principles." *Problems of Postcommunism*. Forthcoming, https://doi.org/10.1080/10758216.2021.1931339.

Akhmednabiev, A. 2011. "Kebedov: In Dagestan Not a Single Real Militant has Passed through the Commission on Adaptation," *Kavazsky Uzel*, December 11. : www.kavkaz-uzel.eu/articles/197442/.

Aliyev, H. 2019. "The Logic of Ethnic Responsibility and Progovernment Mobilization in East Ukraine Conflict." *Comparative Political Studies*, 52 (8), 1200–1231.

Allison, R. 2013. *Russia, The West and Military Intervention*. Oxford: Oxford University Press.

Anishchuk, A. 2011. "Suicide Bomber Kills 35 at Russia's Biggest Airport" *Reuters*, January 24. www.reuters.com/article/us-russia-blast-airport/suicide-bomber-kills-35-at-russias-biggest-airport-idUSTRE70N2TQ20110124.

Arjona, A. 2016. *Rebelocracy*. New York: Cambridge University Press.

Arjona, A. 2017. "Civilian Cooperation and Non-Cooperation with Non-State Armed Groups: The Centrality of Obedience and Resistance." *Small Wars & Insurgencies*, 28(4–5), 755–778.

Aronow, P. M., A. Coppock, F. W. Crawford, and D. P. Green. 2013. "Combining List Experiment and Direct Question Estimates of Sensitive Behavior Prevalence." *arXiv preprint*: 1312.1268.

Aronson, E., T. D. Wilson, and M. B. Brewer. 1998. "Experimentation in Social Psychology." In *Handbook of Social Psychology*, ed. G. Lindzey and E. Aronson. 2nd ed. New York: Random House, pp. 99–142.

Arreguin-Toft, I. 2005. *How the Weak Win Wars: A Theory of Asymmetric Conflict*. New York: Cambridge University Press.

Bakke, K. M., J. O'Loughlin, G. Toal, and M. Ward, 2014. "Convincing State-Builders? Disaggregating Internal Legitimacy in Abkhazia." *International Studies Quarterly*, 58(1), 591–607.

Balcells, L. 2010. "Rivalry and Revenge: Violence against Civilians in Conventional Civil Wars." *International Studies Quarterly*, 54(2), 291–313.

Balcells, L. and S. N. Kalyvas. 2014. "Does Warfare Matter? Severity, Duration, and Outcomes of Civil Wars." *Journal of Conflict Resolution*, 58 (8), 1390–1418. doi:10.1177/0022002714547903.

Bar-Anan, Y., N. Liberman, and Y. Trope. 2006. "The Association between Psychological Distance and Construal Level: Evidence from an Implicit Association Test." *Journal of Experimental Psychology: General*, 135(4), 609.

Barter, S. J. 2017. "Civilian Strategy Across Southeast Asia." *Journal of Peacebuilding & Development*, 12(3), 98–103.

BBC Monitoring. 2012. "Press Gloom on Theatre Siege." BBC Monitoring. http://news.bbc.co.uk/2/hi/europe/3207319.stm.

BBC News. 2010. "Militants hit Russia Power Plant, Killing Two Guards." BBC News, July 21. www.bbc.co.uk/news/world-europe-10708389.

BBC News. 2010. "Moscow Metro Hit by Deadly Suicide Bombings." *BBC News*, March 29. http://news.bbc.co.uk/2/hi/8592190.stm.

Beath, A., F. Christia, and R. Enikolopov. 2017. Can Development Programs Counter Insurgencies? Evidence from a Field Experiment in Afghanistan, MIT Working Paper No. 2011–14. https://papers.ssrn.com/sol3/papers.cfm?abstract_id=1809677.

Benstead, L. J. 2014. "Effects of Interviewer–Respondent Gender Interaction on Attitudes toward Women and Politics: Findings from Morocco." *International Journal of Public Opinion Research*, 26(3), 369–383.

Berman, E., J. Shapiro, and J. Felter. 2011. "Can Hearts and Minds Be Bought? The Economics of Counterinsurgency in Iraq." *Journal of Political Economy*, 119: 766–819.

Bernard, H. R, E. C. Johnsen, P. D. Killworth, and S. Robinson. 1989. "Estimating the Size of an Average Personal Network and of an Event Subpopulation." In *The Small World*, ed. M. Kochen. Norwood, NJ: Ablex, pp. 159–175.

Bernard, H. R, E. C. Johnsen, P. D. Killworth, and S. Robinson. 1991. "Estimating the Size of an Average Personal Network and of an Event Subpopulation: Some Empirical Results." *Social Science Research*, 20, 109–121.

Besley, T. and T. Persson. 2011. "Fragile States and Development Policy." *Journal of the European Economic Association*, 9: 371–398.

Blair, G. 2020. "Survey Methods for Sensitive Topics." *APSA Comparative Politics Newsletter*.

Blair, G., A. Coppock, and M. Moor. 2020. "When to Worry about Sensitivity Bias: A Social Reference Theory and Evidence from 30 Years of List Experiments." *American Political Science Review*, 114(4): 1297–1315.

Blair, G., C. Fair, N. Malhotra, and J. Shapiro. 2013. "Poverty and Support for Militant Politics: Evidence from Pakistan." *American Journal of Political Science* 57(1), 30–48.

Blair, G. and K. Imai. 2012. "Statistical Analysis of List Experiments." *Political Analysis*, 20, 47–77.

Blair, G., K. Imai, and J. Lyall. 2014. "Comparing and Combining List and Endorsement Experiments: Evidence from Afghanistan." *American Journal of Political Science*, 58(4), 1043–1063.

Blair, G., K. Imai, and Y. Y. Zhou. 2015. "rr: Statistical Methods for the Randomized Response Technique." Available at CRAN: https://cran.r-pro ject.org/package=rr.

Blattman, C. and E. Miguel. 2010. "Civil War." *Journal of Economic Literature*, 48(1), 3–57.

Blaydes, L. and R. Gillum. 2013. "Religiosity-of-Interviewer Effects: Assessing the Impact of Veiled Enumerators on Survey Response in Egypt." *Politics and Religion*, 6(3), 459–482.

Brewer, M. 1999. "The Psychology of Prejudice: Ingroup Love and Outgroup Hate?" *Journal of Social Issues*, 55(3), 429–444.

Bullock, W., K. Imai, and J. N. Shapiro. 2011. "Statistical Analysis of Endorsement Experiments." *Political Analysis*, 19, 363–384.

Bustikova, L. 2019. *Extreme Reactions: Radical Right Mobilization in Eastern Europe*. New York: Cambridge University Press.

Bustikova, L. and C. Corduneanu-Huci. 2017. "Patronage, Trust and State Capacity: The Historical Trajectories of Clientelism." *World Politics*, 69(2), 277–326.

Campaign for Innocent Victims in Conflict. 2010a. Addressing Civilian Harm in Afghanistan: Policies and Practices of International Forces. White paper. New York: CIVIC. https://civiliansinconflict.org/wp-content/uploads/2017/ 10/Addressing_civilian_harm_white_paper_2010.pdf.

Campaign for Innocent Victims in Conflict. 2010b. United States Military Compensation to Civilians in Armed Conflict. White paper. New York: CIVIC. https://civiliansinconflict.org/publications/policy/united-states-mili tary-compensation-civilians-armed-conflict/.

Campana, A. and J. F. Ratelle. 2014. "A Political Sociology Approach to the Diffusion of Conflict from Chechnya to Dagestan and Ingushetia." *Studies in Conflict & Terrorism*, 37(2), 115–134.

Campbell, S. P. 2017. "Ethics of Research in Conflict Environments." *Journal of Global Security Studies*, 2(1), 89–101.

Chaiken, S. 1980. "Heuristic Versus Systematic Information Processing and the Use of Source Verus Message Cues in Persuasion." *Journal of Personality and Social Psychology*, 39(5),752–766.

Chaisty, P. and S. Whitefield. 2017. "Understandings of the Nation in Russian Public Opinion: Survey Evidence from Putin's Russia (2001–2014)." *Russian Politics*, 2(2), 123–154.

Chaudhuri, A. and T. Christofides. 2007. Item Count Technique in Estimating the Proportion of People with a Sensitive Feature. *Journal of Statistical Planning and Inference*, 137, 589–593.

Chaudhuri, A. and T. Christofides. 2013. *Indirect Questioning in Sample Surveys*. Berlin: Springer Science & Business Media.

Chivers, C. J. 2007. "The School" *The Esquire*, March 14. www.esquire.com/features/ESQ0606BESLAN_140.

Cialdini, R. B. 1984. *Influence: The New Psychology of Modern Persuasion*. New York: Harper Collins.

Collombier, V. and O. Roy, eds. 2018. *Tribes and Global Jihadism*. New York: Oxford University Press.

Condra, L., and J. Shapiro. 2012. "Who Takes the Blame? The Strategic Effects of Collateral Damage." *American Journal of Political Science*, 56(1), 167–187.

Corstange, D. 2009. "Sensitive Questions, Truthful Answers? Modeling the List Experiment with LISTIT." *Political Analysis*, 17(1), 45–63.

Cronin-Furman, K. and M. Lake. 2018. "Ethics Abroad: Fieldwork in Fragile and Violent Contexts." *PS: Political Science& Politics*, 51(3), 607–614.

Crost, B., J. Felter, and P. Johnston. 2014. "Aid under Fire: Development Projects and Civil Conflict." *American Economic Review*, 104(6), 1833–1856.

Derlugian, G. 1999. "Che Guevaras in Turbans: The Twisted Lineage of Islamic Fundamentalism in Chechnya and Dagestan," *New Left Review*, Vol. A, No. 237, 3–27.

Downes, A. 2008. *Targeting Civilians in War*. Ithaca, NY: Cornell University Press.

Druckman, J. N., D. P. Green, J. H. Kuklinski, and A. Lupia. 2006. "The Growth and Development of Experimental Research in Political Science." *American Political Science Review*, 100(4), 627–635.

Druckman, J. N., D. P. Green, J. H. Kuklinski, and A. Lupia. 2011. *Cambridge Handbook of Experimental Political Science*. New York: Cambridge University Press.

Dunning, T. 2012. *Natural Experiments in the Social Sciences: A Design-Based Approach*. New York: Cambridge: Cambridge University Press.

Dzutsati, V. 2020. "Despite Demise of Insurgency, Authorities Still Wary of Its Remnants." *The Jamestown Foundation, Eurasia Daily Monitor*, May 20. https://jamestown.org/program/despite-demise-of-insurgency-in-north-caucasus-russian-authorities-still-wary-of-its-remnants/.

Dzutsati, V., D. Siroky, and K. Dzutsev. 2016. "The Political Economy of Support for Sharia: Evidence from the Russian North Caucasus." *Politics and Religion*, 9(4), 695–719.

Eriksen, C. W. 1960. "Discrimination and Learning Without Awareness: A Methodological Survey and Evaluation." *Psychological Review*, 67(5), 279.

Fair, C.C. and B. Shepherd. 2006. "Who Supports Terrorism? Evidence from Fourteen Muslim Countries." *Studies in Conflict & Terrorism*, 29(1), 51–74.

Findley, M. and S. Edwards. 2007. "Accounting for the Unaccounted: Weak-Actor Social Structure in Asymmetric Wars." *International Studies Quarterly*, 51(3), 583–606.

Fjelde, H. and D. Nilsson. 2018. "The Rise of Rebel Contenders: Barriers to Entry and Fragmentation in Civil Wars." *Journal of Peace Research*, 55(5), 551–565.

Foxall, A. 2013. "A Contested Landscape: Monuments, Public Memory, and Post-Soviet Identity in Stavropol', Russia." *Communist and Post-Communist Studies*, 46(1), 167–178.

Frye, T., S. Gehlbach, K. L. Marquardt, and O. J. Reuter. 2017. "Is Putin's Popularity Real?" *Post-Soviet Affairs*, 33(1), 1–15, DOI: 10.1080/1060586X.2016.1144334.

Fuller, Liz. 2014. "Insurgency Commanders Divulge Details Of Umarov's Death" *Radio Free Europe/Radio Liberty*, July 23. www.rferl.org/a/insurgency-commanders-divulge-of-umarovs-death/25467747.html.

Gaines, B. J., J. H. Kuklinski, and P. J. Quirk. 2007. "The Logic of the Survey Experiment Reexamined." *Political Analysis*, 15(Winter), 1–20.

Gerring, J. and L. Cojocaru. 2016. "Selecting Cases for Intensive Analysis: A Diversity of Goals and Methods." *Sociological Methods & Research*, 45 (3), 392–423.

Gingerich, D. W. 2010. "Understanding Off-the-Books Politics: Conducting Inference on the Determinants of Sensitive Behavior with Randomized Response Surveys." *Political Analysis*, 18: 349–80.

Glynn, A.N. 2013. "What Can We Learn with Statistical Truth Serum? Design and Analysis of the List Experiment." *Public Opinion Quarterly*, 77(S1), 159–172.

Gold, D. 2004. "Hatred's Kingdom: How Saudi Arabia Supports the New Global Terrorism." Washington, DC: Regnery Publishing.

Greenberg, B. G., et al. 1969. "The Unrelated Question Randomised Response Model: Theoretical Framework." *Journal of the American Statistical Association*, 64 (326), 520–539.

Gregson, S., T. Zhuwau, J. Ndlovu, and C. Nyamukapa. 2002. Methods to Reduce Social Desirability Bias in Sex Surveys in Low-development Settings: Experience in Zimbabwe. *Sexually Transmitted Diseases*, 29(10), 568–575.

Gubler, J. R. and J. S. Selway. 2012. "Horizontal Inequality, Crosscutting Cleavages, and Civil War." *Journal of Conflict Resolution*, 56(2), 206–232.

Gurr, T. R. 1970. *Why Men Rebel*. Princeton, NJ: Published for the Center of International Studies, Princeton University [by] Princeton University Press.

Gutterman, S. 2012. "Son of Late Chechen Warlord Reported Killed in Syria." *Reuters*, August 23. www.reuters.com/article/us-syria-crisis-russia-chechen/son-of-late-chechen-warlord-reported-killed-in-syria-idUSBRE87M0RD 20120823.

Hahn, G. M. 2011. *Getting the Caucasus Emirate Right*, Center for Strategic and International Studies Russia and Eurasia Program Report, September 2011, http://csis.org/files/publication/110930_Hahn_GettingCaucasus EmirateRt_Web.pdf.

Hale, H. 2008. *The Foundations of Ethnic Politics: Separatism of States and Nations in Eurasia and the World*. New York: Cambridge University Press.

Hazelton, J. L. 2017. "The Hearts and Minds Fallacy: Violence, Coercion, and Success in Counterinsurgency Warfare." *International Security*, 42(1), 80–113.

Hechter, D. 1988. *Principles of Group Solidarity*. Berkeley, CA: University of California Press.

Hewstone, M., M. Rubin, and H. Willis. 2002. "Intergroup Bias." *Annual Review of Psychology*, 53, 575–604.

Hirose, K., K. Imai, and J. Lyall. 2017. "Can Civilian Attitudes Predict Insurgent Violence? Ideology and Insurgent Tactical Choice in Civil War." *Journal of Peace Research*, 54(1), 47–63.

Hirschman, A. 1970. *Exit, Voice, Loyalty*. Cambridge, MA: Harvard University Press.

Holland, E. C. and J. O'Loughlin. 2010. "Ethnic Competition, Radical Islam, and Challenges to Stability in the Republic of Dagestan." *Communist and Post-Communist Studies*, 43(3), 297–308.

Honaker, J., G. King, and M. Blackwell. 2011. "Amelia II: A Program for Missing Data." *Journal of Statistical Software*, 45(7), 1–47. www.jstatsoft .org/v45/i07/.

Horvitz, D.G., B. V. Shah, and W. R. Simmons. 1967. "The Unrelated Question Randomized Response Model." *Proceedings of the American Statistical Association: Social Statistics Section*, 64(326), 520–539.

Human Rights Center "Memorial." 2012. "Dagestan: Extrajudicial Executions Continue," February 21, https://memohrc.org/ru/news/dagestan-vnesudeb nye-kazni-prodolzhayutsya.

Human Rights Watch. 2015. "Invisible War: Russia's Abusive Response to the Dagestan Insurgency." June 18, www.hrw.org/report/2015/06/18/invisible-war/russias-abusive-response-dagestan-insurgency.

Humphreys, M. and J. Weinstein. 2009. "Field Experiments and the Political Economy of Development." *Annual Review of Political Science*, 12: 367–378.

Ibragimov, M. R. and K. Matsuzato. 2014. "Contextualized Violence: Politics and Terror in Dagestan." *Nationalities Papers*, 42(2), 286–306.

Imai, K. 2011. Multivariate Regression Analysis for the Item Count Technique. *Journal of the American Statistical Association*, 106: 407–416.

Isaev, T. and K. Gadzhieva. 2012. "In Dagestan the Commission on Adaptation of Fighters Considered 46 Applications in Two Years," *Kavkazsky Uzel*, November 2, www.kavkaz-uzel.eu/articles/215088/.

Juarez, F., J. Cabigon, and S. Singh. 2010. "The Sealed Envelope Method of Estimating Induced Abortion: How Much of an Improvement?" in *Methodologies for Estimating Abortion Incidence and Abortion-Related Morbidity: A Review*, ed. S. Singh, L. Remez, and A. Tartaglione. New York: Guttmacher Institute; and Paris: International Union for the Scientific Study of Population, pp. 107–124.

Kalyvas, S. 2006. *The Logic of Violence in Civil War*. Cambridge.

Kalyvas, S. and M. A Kocher. 2007. "How 'Free' is Free-Riding in Civil War? Violence, Insurgency, and the Collective Action Problem." *World Politics*, 59 (2), 177–216.

Kalyvas, S., and L. Balcells. 2010. "International System and Technologies of Rebellion: How the End of the Cold War Shaped Internal Conflict." *American Political Science Review*, 104(3), 415–429.

Kapiev, I. 2020. "Visitors to the Mosque in Makhachkala Voiced Problems Related to Profiling." *Kavkazsky Uzel*, March 6. www.kavkaz-uzel.eu/art icles/346781/.

Kapiszewski, D., L. M. MacLean, and B. L. Read, 2015. *Field Research in Political Science: Practices and Principles*. New York: Cambridge University Press.

Kaplan, O. 2017. *Resisting War: How Communities Protect Themselves*. New York: Cambridge University Press.

Kavkazsky Uzel. 2016. "Killings of Islamic Figures in the North Caucasus (2009-2016)," December 16. www.kavkaz-uzel.eu/articles/244966/.

Kavkazsky Uzel. 2017. "The Ministry of Internal Affairs counted over a thousand Dagestanis in the ranks of IS in Syria," January 31. www .kavkaz-uzel.eu/articles/296890/.

Kilcullen, D. 2009. *The Accidental Guerrilla: Fighting Small Wars in the Midst of a Big One*. New York: Oxford University Press.

Kisriev, E. F. 2007. *Islam v. Dagestane*. Moskva: Logos.

Knobloch-Westerwick, S., B. K. Johnson, and A. Westerwick. 2015. "Confirmation Bias in Online Searches: Impacts of Selective Exposure

Before an Election on Political Attitude Strength and Shifts." *Journal of Computer-Mediated Communication*, 20(2), 171–187.

Kocher, M. A., T. B. Pepinsky, and S. N. Kalyvas. 2011. "Aerial Bombing and Counterinsurgency in the Vietnam War." *American Journal of Political Science*, 55(2), 201–218.

Kolosov, V. A., and A. B. Sebentcov. 2014. 'Severnyi Kavkaz v rossiiskom geopoliticheskom diskurse.' *Polis*, 2, 146–163

Kosta, S. 2019. "Biased Information Networks." *Nature Human Behavior* 3, 1040.

Kreuger, A. and J. Malečková. 2003. "Education, Poverty and Terrorism: Is There a Causal Connection?" *Journal of Economic Perspectives*, 17(4), 119–144.

Lamb, C. W., and D. E. Stem. 1978. "An Empirical Validation of the Randomized Response Technique." *Journal of Marketing Research*, 15: 616–621.

Lazarev, E. 2019. "Laws in Conflict: Legacies of War, Gender, and Legal Pluralism in Chechnya." *World Politics*, 71(4), 667–709.

Lazarev, E and A. Biryukova. 2016. Are Russia's 20 Million Muslims Seething about Putin Bombing Syria? *The Monkey Cage / The Washington Post*. March 7.

Lensvelt-Mulders, G. J. L. M., J. Hox, P. G. M. van der Heijden, and C. J. M. Maas. 2005. "Meta-Analysis of Randomized Response Research." *Sociological Methods and Research*, 33: 319–348.

Levy Paluck, E. 2010. "The Promising Integration of Qualitative Methods and Field Experiments." *Annals of the American Academy of Political and Social Science*, 628: 59–71.

Liberman, N., M. D. Sagristano, and Y. Trope, 2002. "The Effect of Temporal Distance on Level of Mental Construal." *Journal of Experimental Social Psychology*, 38(6), 523–534.

Liberman, N., Y. Trope, and E. Stephan. 2007. "Psychological Distance." In *Social Psychology: Handbook of Basic Principles*, ed. Arie. W. Kruglanski and Tory. E. Higgins. New York: Guilford Press, pp. 353–383.

Lieberman, E. S. 2005. "Nested Analysis as a Mixed-Method Strategy for Comparative Research." *American Political Science Review*, 99: 435–452.

Linke, A. M. and J. O'Loughlin. 2015. "Reconceptualizing, Measuring and Evaluating Distance and Context in the Study of Conflicts: Using Survey Data from the North Caucasus in Russia." *International Studies Review*, 17 (1), 1–19.

Linke A. M., F. D. W. Witmer, J. O'Loughlin, J. T. McCabe, and J. Tir. 2018. "Drought, Local Institutional Contexts, and Support for Violence in Kenya." *Journal of Conflict Resolution*, 62(7), 1544–1578.

Locander, W. B., S. Sudman, and N. M. Bradburn. 1976. "An Investigation of Interview Method, Threat, and Response Distortion." *Journal of the American Statistical Association*, 71, 269–275.

Lyall, J. 2009. "Does Indiscriminate Violence Incite Insurgent Attacks? Evidence from Chechnya." *The Journal of Conflict Resolution*, 53(3), 331–362.

Lyall, J., G. Blair, and K. Imai. 2013. "Explaining Support for Combatants during Wartime: A Survey Experiment in Afghanistan." *American Political Science Review*, 107(4), 679–705.

Magomedov, R. 2020. "Chechen SC refuses to Rehabilitate Dagestani Residents Killed by Law Enforcers," *Kavkazsky Uzel*, March 10. www.eng .kavkaz-uzel.eu/articles/50253/.

Matanock, A. M. and M. García-Sánchez. 2018. "Does Counterinsurgent Success Match Social Support? Evidence from a Survey Experiment in Colombia." *The Journal of Politics*, 80(3), 800–814.

McDermott, R. 2002. "Experimental Methods in Political Science." *Annual Review of Political Science*, 5, 31–61.

Merom, G. 2003. *How Democracies Lose Small Wars: State, Society, and the Failures of France in Algeria, Israel in Lebanon, and the United States in Vietnam*. New York: Cambridge University Press.

Middle East Eye.2015. "IS Claims Deadly Shooting in Russia's Caucasus: SITE." *Middle East Eye*, December 31. www.middleeasteye.net/fr/news/ claims-deadly-shooting-russias-caucasus-site-1293027991.

Miguel, E., S. Satyanath, and E. Sergenti. 2004. "Economic Shocks and Civil Conflict." *Journal of Political Economy*, 112(4),725–753.

Miller, J. D. 1984. A New Survey Technique for Studying Deviant Behavior [PhD thesis]. The George Washington University.

Mironova, V. and S. Whitt. 2018. "Social Norms after Conflict Exposure and Victimization by Violence: Experimental Evidence from Kosovo," *British Journal of Political Science*, 48(3), 749–765.

Mosinger, E. S. 2018. "Brothers or Others in Arms? Civilian Constituencies and Rebel Fragmentation in Civil War." *Journal of Peace Research*, 55(1), 62–77.

Mutz, D. C. 2011. *Population-based Survey Experiments*. Princeton, NJ: Princeton University Press.

Naylor, F. and J. O'Loughlin. 2020. "Who are the "Don't Knows"? Missing Data in Surveys of Post-Soviet Conflict-affected Regions." *Europe Asia Studies*, DOI: 10.1080/09668136.2020.1808192.

Nickerson, R. S. 1998. "Confirmation Bias: A Ubiquitous Phenomenon in Many Guises." *Review of General Psychology*, 2(2), 175–220.

Oleinik, A. 2016. "Corruption on the Road: A Case Study of Russian Traffic Police." *IATSS Research*, 40(1), 19–25.

O'Loughlin, J., E. Holland, and F. Witmer. 2011. "The Changing Geography of Violence in the North Caucasus of Russia, 1999–2011." *Eurasian Geography and Economics*, 52(5), 596–630.

"On the Prohibition of Wahhabi and Other Extremist Activities in the Territory of the Republic of Dagestan." Law of Republic of Dagestan #15, September 22, 1999, http://docs.cntd.ru/document/802037545.

Park, D., A. Gelman, and J. Bafumi. 2017. "Bayesian Multilevel Estimation with Poststratification: State-Level Estimates from National Polls." *Political Analysis*, 12(4), 375–385.

Parkinson, S. E. 2013. "Organizing Rebellion: Rethinking High-risk Mobilization and Social Networks in War." *American Political Science Review*, 107(3), 418–432.

Petty, R. E., J. T. Cacioppo and D. Schumann. 1983. "Central and Peripheral Routes to Advertising Effectiveness: The Moderating Role of Involvement." *Journal of Consumer Research*, 10(2), 135–146.

Plummer, M. 2009. JAGS: Just Another Gibbs Sampler. https://sourceforge.net/projects/mcmc-jags/.

Raghavarao, D. and W. T. Federer. 1979. "Block Total Response as an Alternative to the Randomized Response Method in Surveys." *Journal of the Royal Statistical Society, Series B: Methodological*, 41(1), 40–45.

Ratelle, J. F. 2016. "Caucasian Foreign Fighters in Syria and Iraq: Understanding the Threat of Returnees in the North Caucasus" *Caucasus Survey*, 4(3), 218–238.

Ratelle, J. F. and E. A. Souleimanov. 2017. "Retaliation in Dagestan: The Missing Link in the Mobilization Scheme." *Terrorism and Political Violence*, 29(4), 573–592.

Roggio, B. and A. Gutowski. 2020. "Mapping Taliban Control in Afghanistan." *FDD's Long War Journal.* www.longwarjournal.org/mapping-taliban-control-in-afghanistan.

Romeo, C. and B. Sopher, 1999. "Learning and Decision Costs in One-Person Games." *Journal of Applied Econometrics*, 14(4), 335–357.

Rosenfeld, B., K. Imai, and J. Shapiro. 2016. "An Empirical Validation Study of Popular Survey Methodologies for Sensitive Questions." *American Journal of Political Science*, 60(3), 783–802.

Rozanova, M. S. and A. A. Yarlykapov. 2014. "The Islamic Religion and Cultural Diversity in Contemporary Russia: Case Study of North Caucasus Region, Dagestan." *OMNES: The Journal of Multicultural Society*, 5(1), 22–47.

Rozenas, A. and Zhukov, Y. 2019. "Mass Repression and Political Loyalty: Evidence from Stalin's 'Terror by Hunger'." *American Political Science Review*, 113(2), 569–583.

Rubin, D. B. 1980. "Comment." *Journal of the American Statistical Association*, 75, 591–593.

Russian Criminal Code, www.consultant.ru/document/cons_doc_LAW_10699/ c2877fe51a75f612e1df0f008c620980638457ba/.

Sagramoso, D. 2012. "The Radicalisation of Islamic Salafi Jamaats in the North Caucasus: Moving Closer to the Global Jihadist Movement?" *Europe-Asia Studies*, 64(3), 561–595.

Salehyan, I., D. Siroky and R. Wood. 2014. "External Rebel Sponsorship and Civilian Abuse: A Principal-Agent Analysis of Wartime Atrocities," *International Organization*, 68(3), 663–661.

Sambanis, N. 2005. "Poverty and the Organization of Political Violence: A Review and Some Conjectures." In *Brookings Trade Forum 2004*, ed. Susan M. Collins and Carol Graham, Washington, DC: Brookings Institution, 2005, pp. 165–222.

Savage, S. J. and D. M. Waldman. 2008. "Learning and Fatigue During Choice Experiments: A Comparison of Online and Mail Survey Modes." *Journal of Applied Econometrics*, 23(3), 351–371.

Schaefer, R.W. 2010. *The Insurgency in Chechnya and the North Caucasus: From Gazavat to Jihad*. Santa Barbara, CA: ABC-CLIO, Praeger Security

Seawright, J. 2016. *Multi-Method Social Science: Combining Qualitative and Quantitative Tools*. New York: Cambridge University Press.

Seawright, J. 2021. "What Can Multi-Method Research Add to Experiments?" in *Advances in Experimental Political Science*, ed. J. N. Druckman and D. P. Green. New York: Cambridge University Press, pp. 383–399.

Shadish, W., T. D. Cook, and D. T. Campbell. 2002. *Experimental and Quasi-experimental Designs for Generalized Causal Inference*. Boston, MA: Houghton Mifflin.

Shafiq, N. M. and A. H. Sinno. 2010. "Education, Income, and Support for Suicide Bombings: Evidence from Six Muslim Countries." *Journal of Conflict Resolution*, 54(1), 146–178.

Shakhbanov, M. 2012. "Russians, Azeris, Highlanders: Why are the Results of the Dagestan Census Distorted?" *Regnum*, February 10. https://regnum.ru/ news/polit/1497900.html.

Shapiro J. N. and C. C. Fair. 2009. "Understanding Support for Islamist Militancy in Pakistan." *International Security*, 34(3), 79–118.

Shiraito, Y and K. Imai. 2017. "endorse: Bayesian Measurement Models for Analyzing Endorsement Experiments." R package version 1.6.0. https://CRAN.R-project.org/package=endorse.

Siroky, D. S., and N. Abbasov, 2021. 'Secession and Secessionist Movements' in *Oxford Bibliographies in Political Science*, ed. Sandy Maisel. Oxford: Oxford University Press.

Siroky, D. S. and V. Dzutsev. 2015. "The Empire Strikes Back: Ethnicity, Terrain and Indiscriminate Violence." *Social Science Quarterly*, 96(3), 807–829.

Siroky, D. S., V. Dzutsev, and M. N. Hechter. 2013. "The Differential Demand for Indirect Rule: Evidence from the North Caucasus." *Post-Soviet Affairs*, 29(2), 268–286.

Siroky, D. S., E. A. Souleimanov, J.-F. Ratelle, and M. Popovic. 2021. "Purifying the Religion: An Analysis of Haram Targeting among Salafi Jihadi Groups." *Comparative Politics*, 43(2), 1–29.

Sniderman, P. M. and T. Piazza. 1993. *The Scar of Race*. Boston: Harvard University Press.

Souleimanov, E. A., 2011. "The Caucasus Emirate: Genealogy of an Islamist Insurgency." *Middle East Policy*, 18(4) 155–168.

Souleimanov, E. A. 2018a. "Making Jihad or Making Money? Understanding the Transformation of Dagestan's Jamaats into Organised Crime Groups." *Journal of Strategic Studies*, 41(4), 604–628.

Souleimanov, E. A. 2018b. "A Perfect *Umma*? How Ethnicity Shapes the Organization and Operation of Dagestan's Jihadist Groups." *Ethnicities*, 18(3), 434–453.

Souleimanov, E. A., Abbasov, N., and D. S. Siroky. 2019. "Frankenstein in Grozny: Vertical and Horizontal Cracks in the Foundation of Kadyrov's Rule." *Asia Europe Journal*, 17(1), 87–103.

Souleimanov, E. A. and H. Aliyev. 2015. "Blood Revenge and Violent Mobilization: Evidence from the Chechen Wars." *International Security*, 40(2), 158–180.

Souleimanov, E. A. and D. S. Siroky. 2016. "Random or Retributive?: Indiscriminate Violence in the Chechen Wars." *World Politics*, 68(4), 677–712.

Sriram, C. L., J. C. King, J. A. Mertus, O. Martin-Ortega, J. Herman, and C. Gallaher. 2009. "Researching Repellent Groups: Some Methodological Considerations on How to Represent Militants, Radicals and Other Belligerents," in C. L. Sriram, J. C. King, J. A. Mertus, O. Martin-Ortega, and J. Herman (eds.), *Surviving Field Research: Working in Violent and Difficult Situations*, 127–146, Routledge.

Swensson, B. 1974. Combined Questions: A New Survey Technique for Eliminating Evasive Answer Bias (I) – Basic Theory. Report No. 70 of the Errors in Survey Research Project. Institute of Statistis, University of Stockholm.

Takhasi, K. and H. Sakasegawa. 1977. "A Randomized Response Technique Without Making Use of any Randomizing Device." *Annals of the Institute of Statistical Mathematics*, 29(1), 1–8.

Tessler, M. and H., M. D. 2007. "What Leads Some Ordinary Arab Men and Women to Approve of Terrorist Acts Against the United States?" *Journal of Conflict Resolution*, 51(2), 305–328.

Tiebout, C. 1956. "A Pure Theory of Local Expenditures," *Journal of Political Economy*, 64(5), 416–424.

Toft, M. and Y. M. Zhukov. 2012. "Denial and Punishment in the North Caucasus: Evaluating the Effectiveness of Coercive Counterinsurgency." *Journal of Peace Research*, 49(6), 785–800.

Toft, M. and Y. M. Zhukov. 2015. "Islamists and Nationalists: Rebel Motivation and Counterinsurgency in Russia's North Caucasus." *American Political Science Review*, 109(2), 222–238.

Tracy, P. E., and J. A. Fox. 1981. "The Validity of Randomized Response for Sensitive Measurements." *American Sociological Review*, 46, 187–200.

Transue, J. E., D. J. Lee, and J. H. Aldrich. 2009. "Treatment Spillover Effects across Survey Experiments." *Political Analysis*, 17(Spring), 143–161.

Trinquier, R. 2006. *Modem Warfare: A French View of Counterinsurgency.* Westport: Praeger.

Trope, Y. and N. Liberman. 2003. "Temporal Construal." *Psychological Review*, 110(3), 403–421.

Tsapieva, O. and T. Muslimov, 2000. "Etnopoliticheskaya I etnosocialn -ayasituatsiya v Dagestane I noveyshiekonflikty," *Rossiya I musulmanskiy mir*, 2. Available online at www.ca-c.org/journal/2007-03-eng/14.shtml.

Tsuchiya, T., Y. Hirai, and S. Ono. 2007. "A Study of the Properties of the Item Count Technique." *Public Opinion Quarterly*, 71(Summer), 253– 272.

US Army Field Manual 3–24: Counterinsurgency 2006. Homeland Security Digital Library. www.hsdl.org/?abstract&did=468442.

US Army. 2007. *The US Army/Marine Corps Counterinsurgency Field Manual.* Chicago: University of Chicago Press.

Van Acker, F. 2004. "Uganda and the Lord's Resistance Army: The New Order No One Ordered." *African Affairs*, 103(412), 335–357.

Vatchagaev, M. 2015a. "The Islamic State Is Set to Replace the Caucasus Emirate in the North Caucasus.," *The Jamestown Foundation, Eurasia Daily Monitor*, January 8. https://jamestown.org/program/the-islamic-state-is-set-to-replace-the-caucasus-emirate-in-the-north-caucasus-2/

Vatchagaev, M. 2015b. "What Caused the Demise of the Caucasus Emirate?," *The Jamestown Foundation, Eurasia Daily Monitor*, June 18. https://jamestown.org/program/what-caused-the-demise-of-the-caucasus-emirate-2/.

Ware, R. B. and E. Kisriev. 2001. "Ethnic Parity and Democratic Pluralism in Dagestan: A Consociational Approach," *Europe-Asia Studies*, 53(1), 105–131.

Ware, R. B. and E. Kisriev. 2009. *Dagestan*. North Castle, NY: ME Sharpe.

Ware, R. B. and E. Kisriev, 2010. *Dagestan: Russian Hegemony and Islamic Resistance in the North Caucasus*. London: Routledge.

Ware, R., E. Kisriev, W. Patzelt, and U. Roericht. 2003. "Stability in the Caucasus: The Perspective from Dagestan." *Problems of Post-Communism*, 50, 12–23. DOI: 10.1080/10758216.2003.11656026.

Warner, S.L. 1965. "Randomized Response: A Survey Technique for Eliminating Evasive Answer Bias." *Journal of the American Statistical Association*, 60(March), 63–69.

Weinstein, J. M. 2007. *Inside Rebellion*. New York: Cambridge University Press.

Weller, N., and J. Barnes. 2014. *Finding Pathways: Mixed-Method Research for Studying Causal Mechanisms*. Cambridge: Cambridge University Press.

Wood, E. 2003. *Insurgent Collective Action and Civil War in El Salvador*. New York: Cambridge University Press.

Wood, W. and C. A. Kallgren. 1988. "Communicator Attributes and Persuasion: Recipients' Access to Attitude-Relevant Information in Memory." *Personality and Social Psychology Bulletin*, 14(1), 172–182.

Yarlykapov, A., 2010. "The radicalization of North Caucasian Muslims." In Dannreuther, R., and March, L. Eds. *Russia and Islam: State, Society and Radicalism*. Routledge: New York and London, pp. 137–154.

Zhukov, Y. M. 2011. "Counterinsurgency in a Non-Democratic State: the Russian Example." In *The Routledge Companion to Insurgency and Counter Insurgency*, ed. P.B. Rich and I. Duyvesteyn . London: Routledge.

Zhukov, Y. M., 2012. "Roads and the Diffusion of Insurgent Violence: The Logistics of Conflict in Russia's North Caucasus." *Political Geography*, 31 (3), 144–156.

Zurcher, C. 2007. *The Post-Soviet Wars: Rebellion, Ethnic Conflict, and Nationhood in the Caucasus*. New York: NYU Press.

Acknowledgements

Prior versions were presented at meetings of the Association for the Study of Nationalities, the Association for Slavic, East European, and Eurasian Studies, the Western Political Science Association, the European Consortium for Political Research, and the European Political Science Association. It has also been presented at invited talks at Carlos III Juan March Institute in Spain, the University of Ostrava in the Czech Republic, and the Four Corners Conflict Network, along with internal workshops at the authors' institutions. We are grateful for the insightful feedback we received and would like to thank especially Philip Gamaghelyan, Tomas Hoch, Alexander Kuo, Marlene Laruelle, Egor Lazarev, Brian Mello, Pia Raffler, Jean-Francois Ratelle, Heidi Reynolds-Stenson, Michael Wilson Becerril, Reed Wood, and Thorin Wright. We received tremendously constructive feedback from two anonymous reviewers. In addition, the series editor, James Druckman, offered superb recommendations and sage advice throughout the process. Khasan Dzutsev, may he rest in peace, deserves special thanks for his role in this project. We acknowledge seed funding from the Institute for Social Science Research and the Center for the Study of Religion and Conflict at Arizona State University. Many thanks also to Abdulmanap Nurmagomedov, may he rest in peace, for making Dagestan more widely known internationally in a positive light.

Cambridge Elements $^{\equiv}$

Experimental Political Science

James N. Druckman
Northwestern University

James N. Druckman is the Payson S. Wild Professor of Political Science and the Associate Director of the Institute for Policy Research at Northwestern University. He served as an editor for the journals *Political Psychology* and *Public Opinion Quarterly*, as well as the University of Chicago Press's series in American Politics. He currently is the co-Principal Investigator of Time-Sharing Experiments for the Social Sciences (TESS) and sits on the American National Election Studies' Board. He previously served as President of the American Political Science Association section on Experimental Research and helped oversee the launching of the Journal of Experimental Political Science. He was co-editor of the *Cambridge Handbook of Experimental Political Science*. He is a Fellow of the American Academy of Arts and Sciences and has published more than 100 articles/book chapters on public opinion, political communication, campaigns, research methods, and other topics.

About the Series

There currently are few outlets for extended works on experimental methodology in political science. The new Experimental Political Science Cambridge Elements series features research on experimental approaches to a given substantive topic, and experimental methods by prominent and upcoming experts in the field.

Cambridge Elements ᛜ

Experimental Political Science

Printed in the United States
by Baker & Taylor Publisher Services